Racial & Ethnic Discrimination

Series Editor: Cara Acred

Volume 308

Independence Educational Publishers

First published by Independence Educational Publishers

The Studio, High Green

Great Shelford

Cambridge CB22 5EG

England

© Independence 2017

ISBN-13: 978 1 86168 758 6

Printed in Great Britain

Zenith Print Group

Contents

Introduction

Racial & Ethnic Discrimination is Volume 308 in the **ISSUES** series. The aim of the series is to offer current, diverse information about important issues in our world, from a UK perspective.

ABOUT TITLE

The Race Relations Act was passed by Parliament in Britain in 1976 and Britain is becoming increasingly multicultural. However, racism and ethnic discrimination are continually pervasive problems in our society. In the wake of Brexit in particular, hate crimes in the UK have increased and prejudice is rife in many communities. This book explores the issue of racism, looking at disadvantaged groups, the impact of social media and segregation in today's Britain.

OUR SOURCES

Titles in the **ISSUES** series are designed to function as educational resource books, providing a balanced overview of a specific subject.

The information in our books is comprised of facts, articles and opinions from many different sources, including:

⇨ Newspaper reports and opinion pieces

⇨ Website factsheets

⇨ Magazine and journal articles

⇨ Statistics and surveys

⇨ Government reports

⇨ Literature from special interest groups.

A NOTE ON CRITICAL EVALUATION

Because the information reprinted here is from a number of different sources, readers should bear in mind the origin of the text and whether the source is likely to have a particular bias when presenting information (or when conducting their research). It is hoped that, as you read about the many aspects of the issues explored in this book, you will critically evaluate the information presented.

It is important that you decide whether you are being presented with facts or opinions. Does the writer give a biased or unbiased report? If an opinion is being expressed, do you agree with the writer? Is there potential bias to the 'facts' or statistics behind an article?

ASSIGNMENTS

In the back of this book, you will find a selection of assignments designed to help you engage with the articles you have been reading and to explore your own opinions. Some tasks will take longer than others and there is a mixture of design, writing and research-based activities that you can complete alone or in a group.

Useful weblinks

www.bitc.org.uk

www.blackballad.co.uk

blog.policy.manchester.ac.uk

www.bristol.ac.uk

www.bullying.co.uk

www.childline.org.uk

www.civilrightsmovement.co.uk

www.consented.co.uk

www.theconversation.com

www.equalityadvisoryservice.com

www.equalityhumanrights.com

www.huffingtonpost.co.uk

www.ibtimes.co.uk

www.independent.co.uk

www.theguardian.com

www.leftfootforward.org

www.opinium.co.uk

www.runnymedetrust.org

www.voice-online.co.uk

www.vox.com

workplace.bitc.org.uk

FURTHER RESEARCH

At the end of each article we have listed its source and a website that you can visit if you would like to conduct your own research. Please remember to critically evaluate any sources that you consult and consider whether the information you are viewing is accurate and unbiased.

Chapter 1

Racism & discrimination

Racism

It's illegal to treat people differently because of their race or culture. If it happens to you, remember – no one has the right to make you feel bad or abuse you for who you are.

What is racism?

Racism is when someone's treated differently or unfairly just because of their race or culture. People can also experience prejudice, when a decision is made or opinion formed without knowledge, thought or reason, because of their religion or nationality.

Racism takes many different forms. These can include:

⇨ written or verbal threats or insults

⇨ damage to property, including graffiti

⇨ personal attacks of any kind, including violence

⇨ being treated differently or being excluded because of your race or culture

⇨ having people make assumptions about you because of your race or culture

⇨ people making racist jokes.

Racism can affect anyone. It exists in all races and cultures. If someone is abused or treated unfairly just because of their race, background or culture, this is racism – no matter where they're from.

You can also be affected by racism that isn't directed at you. For example, if you hear someone discriminating against someone else's culture. Even though you're not from that culture, you might still find hearing it offensive.

It's illegal to treat people differently or unfairly because of their race. Nobody has the right to make you feel bad or abuse you. If you're experiencing racial bullying, Childline can help.

Why are some people racist?

Someone who's racist can feel threatened by anyone who is from a different race or culture.

Our views and beliefs develop as we grow up. If you grow up within a family where some members are racist, or have friends who are racist, you may believe that racism is normal and acceptable.

But prejudice of any kind is often based on ignorance and fear of things that are different. Don't fear or dislike what you don't know or understand. Find out more by reading, learning about things online, talking to people and getting lots of different views before you make up your mind.

Imagine being someone else and what this would be like. Think about how you would like to be treated.

Types of racism

Racial discrimination

Racial discrimination is when someone has been treated unfairly because of their race.

It can mean you won't get the same opportunities, respect or support as other people because of your ethnicity. It can also mean people from certain ethnic backgrounds are blocked from achieving their goals in life. Discrimination is illegal.

Sometimes, racial discrimination can happen if there are rules that only affect one racial or religious group. For example, if Jewish boys are not allowed to wear a yarmulke or if a Sikh person is not allowed to wear a turban, this is racial discrimination. However, teachers may ask someone not to wear religious clothing if it's a reasonable request – such as if the clothes could be dangerous to wear during PE.

Sometimes people discriminate against other people without meaning to – this is still wrong.

Racial stereotypes

Stereotypes are used to describe the behaviour of a certain group of people

– such as people from the same race, religion or type of job. Stereotypes are often wrong because they assume that everyone from a certain group acts in the same way.

Racial stereotypes often bring out racist attitudes. Even if it wasn't your intention to be racist, using racial stereotypes can subtly change the way you behave with someone from a different race.

Racist jokes

Even if it's not meant to be offensive, a racist joke can be hurtful to someone and their culture.

A racist joke is still racist. Going along with it gives people the impression that racism is okay.

Sometimes, people make impressions of people from other cultures or tell jokes about different races. If people around you are doing this, it's important to think about whether you want to be a part of it.

Even if someone doesn't show that they're upset at the time, making racist jokes towards them could still be having a negative impact.

Making racist jokes is a form of abuse. Eventually, it will have an impact on how people feel about themselves and their culture.

⇨ The above information is reprinted with kind permission from ChildLine. Please visit www.childline.org.uk for further information.

© ChildLine 2017

Race discrimination and your rights

By Garry Crystal

Since 1976 Britain has had its own laws regarding race discrimination and your rights towards protection under the law. Race discrimination should never be tolerated, and there are legal consequences for those who do discriminate on the grounds of race.

The Race Relations Act 1976

The Race Relations Act 1976 was passed by Parliament in Britain to make acts of racial discrimination unlawful. The act was introduced at a time when Britain was seeing a number of race related acts in major cities such as London and Birmingham. The 1976 act incorporated and updated the original 1965 Race Relations Act that made racial discrimination unlawful in public places. However, the original act was not seen as fair enough as it did not include any rules on employment or housing.

"The Race Relations Act 1976 was passed by Parliament in Britain to make acts of racial discrimination unlawful"

What is Race Discrimination?

Race discrimination can be defined as the act of treating a person less favourably than another on the grounds of race, colour, nationality or ethnic origin. The 1976 act, which was again amended in 2000, means that this type of discrimination is unlawful and there can be legal consequences. There are a number of areas where race discrimination should not occur and rights of individuals are protected and these will include:

⇨ Housing

⇨ Employment – including employment training

⇨ Education

⇨ Public authorities and government agencies

⇨ Prisons

⇨ The provision of goods, services and financial affairs.

Types of race discrimination

Direct discrimination is one of the more unconcealed types of discrimination. It will include acts such as verbal or physical abuse due to a person's colour, nationality or ethnic origin. It can also include issues such as employees being passed over for promotion in the workplace or clubs that operate a quota rule to limit or eliminate black members. With direct discrimination it does not matter whether the discrimination was intended or not. Direct discrimination is unlawful and if proven there can be legal consequences.

Indirect discrimination

Indirect discrimination occurs when, for example, a company has certain rules that apply to everyone but will put certain groups at a disadvantage. For instance a firm that will not employ anyone who does not have a British driving licence. This could be seen as indirect discrimination against foreign nationality workers in the UK. Unlike direct discrimination, employers do have the opportunity to justify their actions if the matter comes to an employment tribunal.

Victimisation and the law

Victimisation is another category that is included in the Race Relations Act. This could occur if someone has brought a claim against a company or an individual and then been treated unfavourably because of this action. It could also apply to a person who has given evidence, for example at an employment tribunal, and then been victimised because of this action. Victimisation should always be brought to the attention of the appropriate authorities and should not be allowed to continue.

Harassment

Harassment is a type of bullying similar to the type seen in school playgrounds. Wherever this type of racial harassment occurs it can have a very detrimental effect on the quality of a person's life. Racial harassment can happen anywhere by anyone, even by public authority figures. Harassment is unlawful on the grounds of national origins, ethnicity and race. However, it is not unlawful on the grounds of colour and nationality.

Enforcing your rights

Racial discrimination, harassment or victimisation should not be tolerated and anyone who has been subjected to this practice should enforce their rights. In employment situations the matter should be taken to a supervisor or Human Resources department. If this does not put an end to the discrimination or a resolution is not found then it could lead to an employment tribunal.

Outside of the working environment there are a number of sources of support such as the Equality and Human Rights Commission*. Lawyers will also be able to give advice on the best course of action to take if race discrimination has occurred. Stamping out racial discrimination will not happen overnight but standing up for your rights is the only way to create a free and equal society.

As the future creators of our society it is very important that young people's rights are enforced if they are infringed upon. Young people can be very vulnerable when it comes to abuse of their rights and they should be made aware of their rights from an early age.

* If you believe you have been discriminated against, contact the Equality Advisory and Support Service on 0808 800 0082 or via their website www.equalityadvisoryservice.com

10 February 2016

⇨ The above information is reprinted with kind permission from Civil Rights Movement. Please visit www.civilrightsmovement.co.uk for further information.

© Civil Rights Movement 2017

Multicultural Britain in the 21st Century

Executive summary from the Opinium report A question of identity and equality in multicultural Britain.

70 years ago in Britain issues of race and identity were unfamiliar to most, in a country that looked very different from today.

However, since then the face of the nation has changed rapidly. Within the lifetime of the baby boomer generation, the UK has gone from a country where almost all communities were single faith and monocultural, to a society where one in ten are ethnic minorities.

The prevailing view about the 1950s through to the 1980s is that we didn't handle this transition particularly well. Each new wave of immigration from another part of the Commonwealth sparked a reaction, often negative, that resulted in rushed legislation to extend restrictions on future entry into Britain. Those who had already arrived often felt targeted by politicians and the authorities – the stop and search powers from the sus laws were particularly resented.

Yet, there is a feeling that since the 1990s the political landscape and social attitudes have changed. This process began slowly with John Major, who made the first tentative steps towards supporting gender, racial and sexual equality. But it was during the premiership of Tony Blair that Britain appeared to become far more at ease with the multicultural society it had become.

Our report looks into whether we truly have become comfortable with the multicultural society we've grown into, from both sides of the divide.

Our insight certainly suggests that we think we have become more tolerant as a country, and this appears to be reflected in the hopes and beliefs of ethnic minorities in the UK.

But these encouraging signs still don't change the fact that some still feel discriminated against. Our report tries to help improve our understanding of multi-ethnic Britain, by exploring our differences as well as our similarities.

Minorities in Britain still suffer discrimination despite progress over the last 20 years

20 years ago earnest attempts to come to terms with Britain as a multiracial society were only just beginning. Just under half (48%) of UK adults think that the United Kingdom has become a less racist country in that time, with a similar proportion of ethnic minorities (46%) agreeing.

However, progress has been limited. Seven in ten (71%) ethnic minorities think that racist beliefs are still widely held in the UK but are not openly

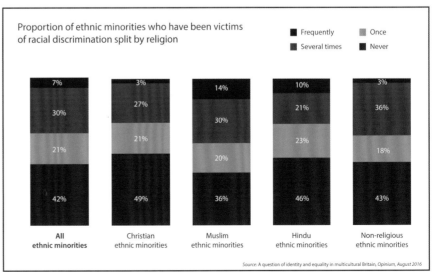

Proportion of ethnic minorities who have been victims of racial discrimination split by religion

■ Frequently ☐ Once ■ Several times ■ Never

	All ethnic minorities	Christian ethnic minorities	Muslim ethnic minorities	Hindu ethnic minorities	Non-religious ethnic minorities
Frequently	7%	3%	14%	10%	3%
Several times	30%	27%	30%	21%	36%
Once	21%	21%	20%	23%	18%
Never	42%	49%	36%	46%	43%

Source: A question of identity and equality in multicultural Britain, Opinium, August 2016

talked about, and 60% believe that racial discrimination is common in the UK. The message is that even if it is less socially acceptable, discrimination on grounds of race has not yet been consigned to the history books.

More than half (58%) of ethnic minorities say that they have been a victim of racial discrimination, while 47% say they have received racially motivated abuse.

One in seven (14%) Muslims and 10% of Hindus frequently face racial discrimination, compared to a handful of ethnic minorities who are Christians. This suggests that some groups are still targeted more than others, and the data at least, should lead us to re-examine the issue of Islamophobia in Britain.

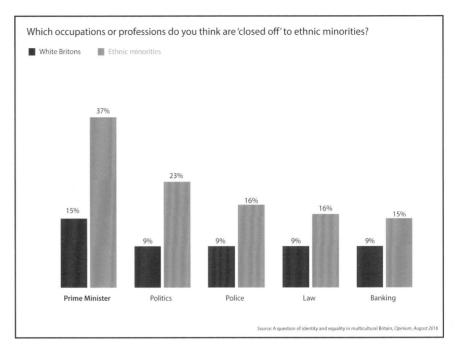

Which occupations or professions do you think are 'closed off' to ethnic minorities?

■ White Britons   ■ Ethnic minorities

Source: A question of identity and equality in multicultural Britain, *Opinium, August 2016*

Racial discrimination is still a problem facing many in Britain

Racial discrimination and abuse is mainly being perpetrated by strangers (64%) as opposed to others known directly to the victims. The most common forms of discrimination or abuse reported by victims support the notion that it is the invectives and prejudices of strangers that affect ethnic minorities the most:

⇨ Insulted directly – 47%

⇨ Receiving end of racist jokes or insults – 40%

⇨ Receiving end of racist stereotyping – 40%

⇨ Treated differently in public places (e.g. shops/restaurants) – 38%.

Although the political weather has changed much in 20 years, the authorities are still seen by some as a source of prejudice. A fifth (20%) of all Black Britons report being viewed with suspicion by the police, and we've seen from earlier studies that their trust in the police is lower than amongst White Britons.

Many still feel their job prospects are affected by their race

More than a quarter (28%) of victims selected their colleagues as a source

of racial prejudice, and 22% said the same about their management or their boss.

In total, 14% of all ethnic minorities report being denied a job or interview because of their race, and 13% report being turned down for a promotion.

White Britons don't see the difficulties that ethnic minorities feel in securing jobs in the key professions or in politics

The problems that face minorities in the workplace extend to how they perceive many of the high profile professions in the UK. Many ethnic minorities feel there are several professions closed off to them including the police (18%), law (16%) and banking (15%).

This problem is particularly acute in politics. More than a third (37%) of ethnic minorities think that the role of prime minister is barred to them, while 23% think this about a career in politics more generally.

In total, two thirds (63%) of ethnic minorities think that there are occupations or professions closed off to them, rising to 71% amongst the younger generation (aged 18-34). However, White Britons as a whole do not share this pessimism, with only 28% believing that there are still professions closed off to ethnic minorities in the UK.

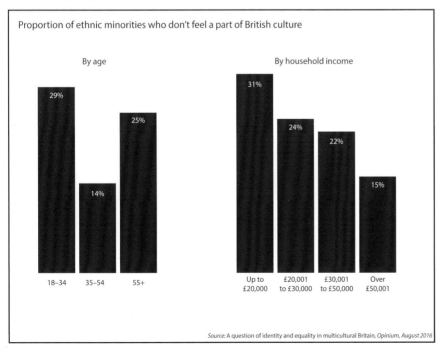

Proportion of ethnic minorities who don't feel a part of British culture

By age

By household income

Source: A question of identity and equality in multicultural Britain, *Opinium, August 2016*

Identity can be complicated for ethnic minorities in modern Britain

Understanding the identity of various groups in society has become a precarious part of multicultural Britain, because our identity is often multifaceted.

Although most of us claim multiple elements to our identity, ranging from our religion to even the local community in which we live, for almost three quarters (72%) of White Britons the country in which they live in is the single most important part of their identity.

However, for many ethnic minorities there are other layers which affect their sense of identity. Although 39% identify most with the country they live in, half consider their religion or ethnicity as the most important part of their identity compared to only 10% of White Britons.

Almost half (47%) of Muslims consider their Islamic faith to be the most important part of their identity, while 43% of Black Britons consider their ethnicity to be the key to describing themselves.

Competing identities impacts on integration and this doesn't show signs of going away

It's important to understand that these competing identities exist in order to begin to tackle many of the problems around integration.

Just over a third (35%) of minorities report feeling like they belong to a different culture, with a further 22% being excluded from society as a whole by explicitly agreeing that they don't feel like they are a part of British culture.

The identity factor plays some role in this. A third (33%) Muslims – the group most likely to identify with their religion – are most likely to say they do not feel a part of British culture, while only 19% of those with no faith feel the same.

However, fundamental issues such as identity are not the only factors in this disconnect from society. A range of socio-economic factors that might not be directly associated with identity come into play. Those with a household income of less than £20,000 a year are twice as likely as those with a household income of more than £50,000 to feel excluded from British culture.

The younger generation are the most likely to say they feel disconnected from British culture (29%), and this is something we should pay attention to if we hope to make progress over the next decade in unifying British citizens.

August 2016

⇨ The above information is reprinted with kind permission from Opinium. Please visit www.opinium.co.uk for further information.

© Opinium 2017

England's most disadvantaged groups: Gypsies, Travellers and Roma

The experiences of Gypsies, Travellers and Roma

Some people in our society are being left further behind because they face particular barriers in accessing important public services and are locked out of opportunities. There are several factors that may contribute to this, including socio-economic deprivation, social invisibility, poor internal organisation of the group, distinctive service needs that are currently not met, cultural barriers, stigma and stereotyping, small group size, and very importantly, a lack of evidence which limits us in our ability to assess the multiple disadvantages these people face.

Although there are many people facing multiple disadvantages in England, here we have focused on the experience of one specific group: Gypsies, Travellers and Roma.

Research published by the Commission in 2009 presented evidence of Gypsies' and Travellers' experience of inequality in a wide range of areas and highlighted "the extent to which many of their experiences remain invisible and ignored within wider agendas" (Cemlyn et al., 2009). Evidence that follows suggests that this is still the case in 2016.

Education

Although the educational attainment of Gypsy, Roma and Traveller children in England improved between 2008/09 and 2012/13, the attainment gap between Gypsy and Roma children, and White pupils appears to have widened, while the gap between Travellers of Irish heritage and White pupils has not changed.

Gypsy, Roma and Traveller children were less likely to achieve "a good level of development" in their early years (EYFS) in 2013/14 (19.1% for Gypsy and Roma children, and 30.9% for Traveller children, compared with 61.8% other White children). Similarly, a lower percentage of Gypsy and Roma children (13.8%) and Traveller children (17.5%) achieved the GCSE threshold in 2012/13 compared with other White children (60.3%) and the attainment gap widened between 2008/09 and 2012/13.

Gypsy, Roma and Traveller children were also among those most likely to be excluded from school. Their exclusion rates were four to five times higher than the national average in 2012/13: Gypsy and Roma (136.3 per 1,000) and Traveller (169.4 per 1,000) children compared with other White children (41.8 per 1,000) in 2012/13.

Gypsy, Roma and Traveller children are particularly vulnerable in a school setting and subjected to bullying (DfE, 2014). Because of the transience of these pupils, head teachers report difficulties in quickly accessing funding; for example, the pupil premium, for new pupils. There was also a shortage of expertise to provide effective support to Roma pupils (Ofsted, 2014).

Work and standard of living

In 2011, Gypsy or Irish Travellers had the lowest recorded economic activity in England and Wales (47% compared with 63%). The most common reason given for those who were economically inactive was looking after the home or family (ONS, 2014). Over half of those who were economically active were employed, and high proportions were looking for work (20% compared with 7% for all adults in England and Wales) or were self-employed (26% compared with 14%). Roma were often in low-paid waged employment, faced discrimination in employment agency work, and worked informally for 'cash in hand' work (Ryder and Cemlyn, 2014).

The Government placed responsibility for the provision of Gypsy and Traveller sites in England with local authorities, on the basis that local authorities were best placed to assess the needs of their communities. The Government provided funding from 2011 to 2015 as part of the Affordable Homes Programme for the provision of new and refurbished Traveller sites, and gave incentives to local authorities through the New Homes Bonus Scheme to provide new housing, including Traveller sites.

However, some local authorities are reluctant to provide new sites or refurbish existing ones, and Gypsies and Travellers face difficulties when applying for planning permission for private sites (Advisory Committee on the Framework Convention for the Protection of National Minorities, 2011). In a recent legal case the Secretary of State for Communities and Local Government was found to have acted unlawfully in Gypsy and Traveller planning applications on green belt land in England, in breach of the Equality Act 2010 and of Article 6 (Moore & Coates v SSCLG [2015] EWHC 44).

There is a twice-yearly count of Traveller caravans, which takes place in January and July. Since 2010, the number of Traveller caravans on unauthorised sites has decreased. The number on authorised private sites has increased and on socially rented sites has remained relatively stable. In January 2015, 20,123 Traveller caravans were counted in England: 6,867 (34%) on socially rented sites and 10,585 (53%) on privately rented sites, with the remainder on unauthorised sites (DCLG, 2015).

Health

Compared with the general population, Gypsies and Travellers are more likely to suffer bad health. This includes lower life expectancy, high infant mortality rates, high maternal mortality rates, low child immunisation levels, higher prevalence of anxiety and depression, chronic cough or bronchitis (even after smoking is taken into account), asthma, chest pain and diabetes (DCLG, 2012), and higher rates of smoking (Aspinall and Mitton, 2014). This is exacerbated by the fact that many Gypsies and Travellers remain unregistered with GPs (RCGP, 2013).

In 2011, 14.1% of Gypsies and Irish Travellers in England and Wales rated their health as bad or very bad, compared with 5.9% of White British and 9.2% of White Irish people (ONS, 2013).

While the variability in general health among different ethnic groups can sometimes be explained by an older age profile, this is not the case for Gypsies and Irish Travellers, of whom only 6% were aged 65 and above in 2011 and who had a low median age of 26 (ONS, 2014). Improved life expectancy of Gypsy and Traveller communities appears to be associated with the availability of established site provision and access to medical care (Cemlyn et al., 2010). A recent report for the Department of Health noted that accommodation insecurity, the conditions of Gypsies' and Travellers' living environment, low community participation and discrimination all play key roles in exacerbating these poor health outcomes (The Traveller Movement, 2016). It suggested that these factors also hold the key to effectively addressing and improving health and well-being. It called for long-term, joined-up working at both local and national level to address the wider social determinants of Gypsies' and Travellers' ill-health.

There is emerging evidence that health inequalities of Roma people are similar to those identified among Gypsies and Travellers, including a high prevalence of diabetes, cardiovascular disease, premature myocardial infarction, obesity, asthma and mental health issues such as stress, anxiety and depression (EC, 2014). Poor familiarity with healthcare provisions and language barriers may make it difficult for them to access health services (EC, 2014; Lane et al., 2014). Cultural norms

may prevent some Roma people from accessing services for support with mental health, sexual health, and drug and alcohol misuse (EC, 2014). Infrequent contact with health providers may also be exacerbating the health problems of some Roma patients (Social Marketing Gateway, 2013).

Although the Department of Health in England pledged in 2012 to identify gaps in data and research, and to highlight interventions that lead to positive health outcomes (in DCLG, 2012), concerns remain about the extent to which NHS services collect data on Gypsy, Traveller and Roma patients (Aspinall, 2014).

Prisons

Gypsies, Roma or Travellers are considerably over-represented in prison. In 2013–14, 4% of the prison population identified as Gypsy, Roma or Traveller in the HMIP prisoner survey, whereas only 0.1% of the population identified as such in the 2011 census (HMIP, 2014).

The exact size of the population in prison is not known because levels of selfreporting were low and the option to record a prisoners' ethnicity as 'Gypsy or Irish Traveller' was only added to the Prison National Offender Management Information System monitoring system for the first time in 2011 (PPO, 2015).

Gypsies, Roma and Travellers were more likely to report feeling unsafe in prison (46%) compared with other prisoners (33%), and more likely to say they had been victimised by other prisoners (36% compared with 23%) and by staff (40% compared with 27%). They were also more likely to report that they been physically restrained or had been in segregation in the previous six months (14% compared with 6%) (HMIP, 2014).

Their vulnerability in prison may further be heightened by separation from their families, high levels of mental illness, lack of adequate mental health support and not being able to read or write (PPO, 2015).

Stigmatising treatment

Negative attitudes towards Gypsy, Roma and Traveller communities were still widely held.

⇨ According to the Spring 2014 Global Attitudes survey, 50% of people in Britain reported having an unfavourable view of Roma (Pew Research Centre, 2014).

⇨ Discrimination and harassment of Gypsies, Roma and Travellers was common across Britain, not only on the part of the general public but also by the police and other authorities (Lane, Spencer and Jones, 2014).

⇨ Evidence from a study carried out in Devon found that some people from Gypsy, Roma and Traveller communities had hidden their ethnic identity in order to access employment and services, and others said their children were bullied at school and that they had been refused entry to pubs and cinemas (Devon and Cornwall Police, 2013).

⇨ Britain has failed to make progress on all of the measures aimed at fighting discrimination that are part of the European Commission's Framework for National Roma Integration (EC, 2013).

Hostility towards individuals and groups on the basis of ethnicity is often channelled through political rhetoric and the media, which has been criticised by human rights monitoring bodies and highlighted by the Leveson Inquiry:

⇨ The Irish Traveller Movement in Britain provided numerous examples of bias, racism and stereotyping in the media in relation to the reporting of Gypsy, Roma and Traveller issues and claimed that it was making the integration of these communities more difficult (Irish Traveller Movement in Britain, 2012).

⇨ There were many examples of 'prejudicial or pejorative references' to particular races or ethnicities in the press. For example, in 2013 an opinion piece in The Spectator described Gypsy, Roma and Traveller people as lazy, criminal and unintelligent. The author Rod Liddle claimed that usage of the terms 'gyppo' and 'pikey' were a "useful means of lumping them all together" (Liddle, 2013).

⇨ Channel 4's series Big Fat Gypsy Weddings has also been found to have perpetuated negative stereotypes. In 2012, the broadcaster was criticised by the Advertising Standards Agency for an advertising campaign which featured posters with the words 'Bigger. Fatter. Gypsier'. The decision that the complaints did not warrant investigation was challenged by the Irish Traveller Movement and eight other complainants, and an independent review of the agency's decision led to the case being re-opened. The Advertising Standards Agency took advice from the EHRC and upheld that the adverts were offensive because they were racist, denigrating and portrayed Gypsies and Travellers in a negatively stereotypical way. It also stated that the adverts were irresponsible because they depicted negative stereotypes of Gypsies and Travellers, and endorsed prejudice against them (Advertising Standards Agency, 2012).

March 2016

⇨ The above information is an extract from the publication *England's most disadvantaged groups: Gypsies, Travellers and Roma*. It is reprinted with kind permission from the Equality and Human Rights Commission. Please visit www.equalityhumanrights. com for further information.

⇨ Adapted from https://www. equalityhumanrights.com/ sites/default/files/ief_gypsies_ travellers_and_roma.pdf. Visit for full references.

⇨ The copyright in the document this publication has been adapted from and all other intellectual property rights in that material are owned by, or licensed to, the Commission for Equality and Human Rights, known as the Equality and Human Rights Commission ("the EHRC").

© Equality and Human Rights Commission 2017

Muslim women and discrimination in Britain

An article from The Conversation.

By Julian Hargreaves, Research Associate at the Centre of Islamic Studies, University of Cambridge

The controversy surrounding a now-infamous "I confronted a Muslim" tweet – and a subsequent race-hate charge – reminds us that tackling discrimination against British Muslims remains as big a challenge as ever.

For those who missed it, PR-man Matthew P Doyle took to Twitter to announce: "I confronted a Muslim woman in Croydon yesterday. I asked her to explain Brussels. She said 'Nothing to do with me'. A mealy mouthed reply."

Police were alerted to the incident when Doyle's ill-judged comments about the encounter were retweeted by bemused Internet users. While charges were eventually dropped, the story is a prime example of the type of discrimination encountered on a daily basis by many British Muslim women and an exception to an otherwise overlooked phenomenon.

Everyday incidents of anti-Muslim discrimination rarely make headline news – but recent research from the University of Cambridge's Centre of Islamic Studies found that discrimination is the daily norm for many British Muslims.

While previous research in this area has often focused on acts of physical violence, none of those interviewed for the Cambridge study had experienced crime of this type. But almost all, whether male or female, felt they had experienced prejudice. As one Muslim man living in the north of England stated: "… there's an atmosphere, there's definitely an atmosphere."

Interviewees shared numerous accounts of being ignored in shops, being stared at on public transport and being targeted by discrimination. While they were seldom criminal in nature, these acts were described as always hurtful – and often leading to dramatically increased fears of criminal victimisation, particularly among older Muslim women.

Muslim voices

One Muslim woman gave an account of discrimination from supermarket staff packing groceries:

"When we're shopping … right away from the person who's serving you … he or she [is] serving someone who's white you get a full conversation out of them, but the minute they see you with a hijab, right okay, pack yourself."

Another gave one of many examples of discrimination on public transport:

"When I'm in my normal get-up … I can sit in the bus like everyone else and I'm fine, people talking away just getting on with it, you know, you'll even find someone sitting next to you trying to strike conversation … wear a hijab and it's almost like … nobody even wants to smile at you … they want to keep at arm's length from you."

These troubling accounts echo previous victim and discrimination studies undertaken by the centre. Analysis of data from the Crime Survey for England and Wales (previously the British Crime Survey) revealed that levels of personal crime (crimes ranging from verbal abuse to serious attack) and crimes including some form of physical violence are broadly similar for all minority religion groups (with the sad exception of Jewish communities who face higher overall levels of crime).

A forthcoming study of discrimination data from the Ethnic Minority British Election Study 2010 (EMBES), a large-scale survey of ethnic minority communities, tells a different overall story. Data from EMBES suggests that non-white Muslims who experience discrimination are more likely than non-white Christians to suffer it on the street – but perhaps no more likely than Hindu and Sikh communities. (Muslim victims may appear to suffer more discrimination on the street than Hindus and Sikhs but the differences are not statistically significant and so should not be used to describe larger national patterns.)

However, there are stark differences between female discrimination victims within the EMBES data. Non-white Muslim women appear far more likely to suffer discrimination on the street than their female non-white, non-Muslim counterparts. These differences are large and statistically significant, therefore provide a more reliable estimate of differences throughout the UK. The experiences shared by female Muslim interviewees in the recent study offered strong support for the statistical evidence.

Visible difference

One probable explanation for the increased risks faced by British Muslim women is of course the higher visibility of those who choose to wear a headscarf or face veil (as many of the interviewees do). Several interviewees drew direct links between daily incidents of discrimination and the abundance of negative news stories concerning Muslims and Islam.

Others (the lucky few perhaps) were careful to stress a growing resilience to everyday forms of discrimination and an increased reliance on their religion, culture and community as a means of coping. This finding of resilience is perhaps the study's most original contribution to academic research in this field.

Regardless of how we might as a society analyse, explain and cope with everyday forms of discrimination (against any individual or group), what the study makes clear is that as the furore around Doyle's crass foray onto Twitter begins to fade, encounters of this sort are happening all over Britain and continue to be for many British Muslims the unreported reality of daily life.

1 April 2016

⇨ The above information is reprinted with kind permission from *The Conversation*. Please visit www. theconversation.com for further information.

White people may deny it, but racism is back in Britain

Discrimination, prejudice, violence and common bigotry raise no concern these days.

By Yasmin Ailbhai-Brown

In 1960, American novelist Harper Lee wrote her masterpiece, *To Kill a Mocking Bird*.

It won the Pulitzer Prize, and was made into a film starring Gregory Peck. Among the central characters is Atticus Finch, a virtuous white lawyer, who defends Tom Robinson, a black man charged with rape.

The novelist wrote at a time when black masculinity was criminalised and innocent men were frequently lynched, framed and executed. Lee exposed the squalid, racist culture of her homeland and found hope in liberal values. Then she fell silent.

Decades passed. In the long-awaited sequel published this week, *Go Set a Watchman*, Finch has become a hard racist and segregationist.

African Americans greeted the new novel with relief.

A good friend, an academic in San Francisco, emailed: "Harper is finally telling the truth. Those guys like Finch, who pretended to be with us, were lying to themselves. They liked to be anti-racist heroes, but only when it suited them. Inside their liberal hearts and heads they are supremacists. My son married the daughter of a lawyer who loved Martin Luther King and all that. He refused to walk her down the aisle. So I did."

He is a businessman, who wants to remain anonymous because he is worried about the consequences of speaking out.

A new American film, *Dear White People*, has just been released in the UK. Witty and caustic, it examines white privilege and black identity. It will pull audiences. We find strange comfort in tut-tutting about racism in America. It makes us feel morally superior.

No black Briton would dare to do something similar. It's fine to make movies about long-ago slaves and the Raj. But to put stories of racially unjust Britain, here and now, on screen? Absolutely not. (Go on, prove me wrong.)

There is much national outrage when well-known people use words that are deemed offensive. But discrimination, prejudice, violence and common bigotry raise no concern these days. People of colour die in custody or during arrest; black graduates are kept out of jobs; apprenticeships are harder to get if you are not white; minorities are more likely to be stopped and searched and new migrants are seen as "cockroaches".

The National Audit Office recently looked at the top civil service and found it to be almost wholly white and male. Researchers have found that ethnic-minority offenders are more likely than white offenders to be sent to prison and get long sentences. Black men and women cannot get into trendy clubs. Colour matters more than talent in almost every profession. Race-discrimination cases are much harder to pursue and most victims have given up trying.

Here she goes again, many readers will think, say, and tweet. Special pleading, guilt-tripping tolerant, white Brits. GET OVER IT. And anyway, the real bigots are black and Asian people, Muslims most of all – they who hate white folk, western culture, our freedoms. Terrorism is the real problem, they say. White working classes suffer more. Racism is so yesterday. Black is the new white.

I wish.

Frankie Boyle is rare among white men. He speaks up again and again against this perfidious, contemporary racism. And, many would say, crosses a line.

Raising this subject causes a bad smell, revulsion and odium. The messengers are denounced and cursed. Denial and complacency fight back.

The nation should be proud of how it has allowed talent to flower. Look at black actors Idris Elba and Chiwetel Ejifor, presenters Mishal Hussein and

Reeta Chakrabarti, MPs Priti Patel, Sajid Javid, Sadiq Khan and David Lammy, novelists Kamla Shamsie and Andrea Levy, actors Mera Syal and Sanjeev Bhaskar – and so on, and on. Yes minorities can now reach for the skies, but most fall to earth, get hurt and lose hope.

Let me try and explain everyday, normative racism and how it works. Think about how people of colour are branded "controversial" when they are assertive; how white deaths matter more than brown or black deaths; how little black kids are called "ugly" in playgrounds, and trolls who attack us for our race and say we do not belong; the way we and our children are constantly asked where we come from; the way the media demonises dark-skinned people and how politicians describe us as trainee citizens on lifelong-learning programmes to become true Brits.

Men write in to tell me black and Asian women are hot and sexy: that is horribly racist, and also sexist. Those who ask me all the time why Muslims won't integrate need to understand the bigotry inherent in that question. I am not responsible for those who live separate lives and choose to harm this nation and its people. The 7/7 bombers killed people of every nationality. I daily damn these ghetto mentalities.

This is not intended as a pessimistic dirge. Great Britain is a vibrant, cosmopolitan, modern nation, where love and friendships flourish between the races and ethnicities. But structural racism is back. The good news cannot offset the bad.

Writer and novelist Hanif Kureishi wrote recently on Enoch Powell's abiding legacy: "Racism is the lowest form of snobbery. Its language mutates: not

long ago, the word 'immigrant' became an insult, a stand in for 'p**i' or 'n****r'... people like Powell, men of ressentiment, with their omens and desires to humiliate, will return repeatedly to divide and create difference."

We have to talk about racism, find words and courage to repeatedly defy malevolence. Easier said than done. Millions of dear, white people get livid, don't want to know or deny the problem. That is why anti-racism is so weak today and why it must get bolder and braver.

12 July 2015

⇨ The above information is reprinted with kind permission from *The Independent*. Please visit www.independent.co.uk for further information.

Revealed: the truth about ethnic diversity of neighbourhoods

An article from **The Conversation.**

THE CONVERSATION

By Aneta Piekut, lecturer in Quantitative Social Sciences, University of Sheffield

In many European countries, people overestimate the share of minority populations and immigration volume. This could be a result of people not being well informed or knowledgeable about the social issues around them. But skewed perceptions of ethnic diversity have implications

for social relations and openness towards minority ethnic groups.

Although the influence of ethnic diversity on various aspects of social life has been thoroughly investigated in many countries, results are still inconclusive. Some studies found that

ethnic diversity is harmful to community cohesion, because it lowers trust in others. Other research says that it promotes better relationships between people of different ethnicities, because it provides more opportunities for everyday contact with people who are different from us.

But whatever the impacts of ethnic diversity, the issue remains that the "actual" ethnic diversity of our neighbourhoods – calculated using census or other data such as immigration statistics – can be very different from our individual perceptions of it.

Perception vs reality

The research I took part in – Living with Difference in Europe – surveyed the attitudes of white British residents in Leeds and Polish residents in Warsaw toward ethnic minorities. Our analysis was based on responses from over 1,000 people in each city.

We asked them to assess the proportion of people "who are of

Young white men have the worst reputation

British attitudes to 48 different ethnic, age and gender groups. Numbers show the average net percentage who say each group has five positive qualities minus is likely to do five negative activities.

Most praised		Most derided	
White woman in her 60s	67%	White man in his 20s	8%
White man in his 60s	64%	Black caribbean man in his 20s	19%
Chinese woman in her 40s	61%	White woman in her 20s	23%
Chinese woman in her 60s	60%	White Australian man in his 20s	27%
Jewish woman in her 60s	59%	Pakistani-born man in his 20s	28%
Jewish man in his 60s	59%	Polish-born man in his 20s	28%

Source: YouGov, December 2015

different ethnic background to them" living in their neighbourhoods. The results were analysed along small area data on actual ethnic diversity, using the 2011 census for Leeds, and the 2002 census for Warsaw.

We had two very interesting findings. First, the study confirmed the positive effects of higher exposure to actual ethnic diversity: residents of ethnically mixed neighbourhoods in Leeds, and people who have daily contact with those of minority ethnic backgrounds in both cities, are more tolerant towards them.

Second, in both cities, we found that the more diverse residents perceive their neighbourhoods to be, the more prejudiced they are towards minority ethnic groups. Importantly, those who perceive their neighbourhood as being diverse are equally prejudiced against ethnic minorities – regardless of whether their area was actually diverse or not. By contrast, those living in areas with a high percentage of non-White British people in Leeds – who do not "notice" this diversity around them – are more tolerant.

This could indicate that in some places, diversity has become so commonplace – and the presence of ethnic minorities so normal – that they do not stick out as visibly different.

Skewing the picture

We also wanted to know whether perceptions of diversity could denote more negative attitudes toward ethnic minorities in some neighbourhoods than others. After all, every neighbourhood has its own unique make-up and history. We looked at changes in the diversity of neighbourhoods in Leeds between 2001 and 2011. Unfortunately, 2011 census data were not available for small areas in Warsaw.

It turns out that residents who perceive high levels of diversity in their neighbourhoods have more prejudiced attitudes towards ethnic minorities when they live in areas that have actually experienced a recent influx of "white other" (non-British) and "mixed" ethnicity residents.

Interestingly, this was not the case for respondents living among new

Cultural/ethnic diversity

REALITY

PERCEPTION

residents of "Black" and "Asian" ethnicity. We suspect that the recent changes in the media's coverage of immigration from Central and Eastern Europe might contribute towards making these newcomers more visible in society.

We also found out that residents who perceive high levels of diversity have more negative attitudes towards ethnic minorities when they are living in neighbourhoods that have had more council housing added recently. High-density council housing is often associated with more disorder, higher levels of violence and fewer opportunities to engage in social life with others. So, we suspect that this may cause residents to feel insecure, and subsequently project these feelings onto local ethnic minority groups – whether or not they are council housing tenants.

Perhaps most importantly, we learned that perceptions of diversity are dynamic across cities – they could be very different between residents living in two similar neighbourhoods in terms of actual proportion of minority

ethnic groups. Both the characteristics of the neighbourhoods, and recent changes in the local population, could be responsible for distorting people's perceptions of ethnic diversity.

Our findings show that we cannot tackle prejudice simply by mixing people of different ethnicities together in the same neighbourhood. Contact between different ethnic groups can help to increasing tolerance. But it seems that peaceful and respectful coexistence can be diminished when our prejudices are reinforced by negative media or social stereotypes.

3 May 2016

⇨ The above information is reprinted with kind permission from *The Conversation*. Please visit www.theconversation.com for further information.

Life is getting worse for young black Britons, research shows

Equality watchdog slams "piecemeal and stuttering" government response.

By Niamh Ní Mhaoileoin

The life chances of young people from ethnic minority backgrounds have gotten much worse over the last five years, according to the biggest ever review of race inequality in Britain.

The research, published by the Equality and Human Rights Commission, shows that long-term unemployment among young BAME people has increased by 49 per cent since 2010, while for white people it has fallen slightly.

Overall unemployment for black people is 12.9 per cent, more than double the rate among white people.

BME people are also less likely to occupy senior professional positions, and are more than twice as likely to be in insecure employment.

And although educational attainment is improving among ethnic minorities, those with degrees are two and a half times more likely to be unemployed than their white counterparts, and earn 23.1 per cent less on average.

BME people are far more likely to be victims of crime, and to be treated more harshly by the criminal justice system – with a rate of prosecution and sentencing three times higher than that of the white population.

Race also remains the most common motivator of hate crime, and the post-Brexit spike raises particular concern.

"The combination of the post-Brexit rise in hate crime and deep race inequality in Britain is very worrying and must be tackled urgently," commented David Issac, chair of the Equality and Human Rights Commission.

"Today's report underlines just how entrenched race inequality and unfairness still is in our society. We must redouble our efforts to tackle race inequality urgently or risk the divisions in our society growing and racial tensions increasing."

Despite welcoming Theresa May's comments on the importance of tackling inequality, Issac criticised the previous government's "piecemeal and stuttering" approach to race equality, accusing it of offering "more one nation platitudes than policies".

The report includes a series of policy recommendations, including the creation of "a comprehensive, coordinated and long-term UK Government strategy with clear and measurable outcomes to achieve race equality."

It also suggests that UK should carry out a full-scale review of hate crime sentencing in England and Wales and take steps to mitigate discriminatory effects of recent access to justice reforms.

It also calls for attention to inequality in police behaviour – a major concern for many BME communities – recommending that monitoring, training and scrutiny be enhanced to ensure that stop-and-search is being used in a lawful and non-discriminatory way.

18 August 2016

⇨ The above information is reprinted with kind permission from Left Foot Forward. Please visit www.leftfootforward.org for further information.

Britain becoming more segregated than 15 years ago, says race expert

Prof. Ted Cantle, who wrote report after 2001 race riots, identifies trends of "more prejudice, intolerance and mistrust" in schools and workplaces.

By Anushka Asthana

British society is increasingly dividing along ethnic lines – with segregation in schools, neighbourhoods and workplaces – that risks fuelling prejudice, according to one of the country's leading experts on race and integration.

"There is more mixing in some parts of our society. But there is also undoubtedly more segregation in residential areas, more segregation in schools and more segregation in workplaces"

Prof. Ted Cantle, who carried out a report into community cohesion in the wake of a series of race riots in 2001, warned that growing divisions had led to mistrust within communities across the country.

Speaking to *The Guardian* 15 years after he called for action to reduce polarisation following violent riots across northern England, in Oldham, Bradford, Leeds and Burnley, Cantle said he was alarmed by the direction the country had headed since then.

"There is more mixing in some parts of our society. But there is also undoubtedly more segregation in residential areas, more segregation in schools and more segregation in workplaces," he said. "That is driving more prejudice, intolerance, mistrust in communities."

Cantle cited as evidence an almost four-fold increase in the number of electoral wards with a non-white majority, from 119 in 2001 to 429 today, saying that suggested communities were more concentrated by race, rather than increasingly mixed. He also pointed out that in the ten years after the riots, London's white-British population was reduced by 600,000, while its minority population rose by 1.2 million, saying that segregation was particularly marked in towns and cities.

Cantle argued that a shift in focus by the previous Labour and then Coalition Government to anti-extremism measures "squeezed out" policies that were meant to promote community cohesion. He claimed that faith schools were particularly problematic, arguing that too many were teaching just one religion or even "manipulating admissions" to cherrypick students.

He also claimed there were deeply segregated workplaces, highlighting food processing and packing as an area of concern. Cantle argued that attempts to make sure employers recruited mixed teams had stalled, leading to too many teams with "single identities".

The academic argued that part of the solution had to be driving a more positive conversation about race in Britain, which accepted that society had changed and tried to focus on the potential benefits of immigration. "We live in a globalised world – we can't disinvent easyJet, we can't undo the internet, we can't turn the clock back on companies being global and we can't undiversify Britain," he said.

It comes as the Labour MP Chuka Umunna issued a similar warning in an article in *The Guardian*. "I believe the cracks in our communities have grown. Not only has Britain become a more ethnically segmented nation as immigration has continued to rise, but also the growing income and lifestyle gap between rich and poor has undermined the sense that there is such a thing as a common British life," he wrote.

Umunna pointed to unrest in London in 2011, arguing that while the city prided itself on diversity, it did not always translate into social interactions between different groups, but instead had constituents "leading parallel lives". The MP is chair of the all-party parliamentary group on integration, which is hearing evidence from Cantle alongside the home office minister Lord Ahmad, and Louise Casey, who is carrying out a major review into integration in Britain.

"We know that people who live in closed communities are more fearful of others and more likely to be prejudiced to people from other backgrounds"

Cantle's comments follow research from the thinktank Demos, which found 61% of ethnic minority children in England, and 90% in London, start year one in schools where the majority of children are from minority groups. The data revealed schools dominated by children of either Bangladeshi, Pakistani or black-Caribbean origin. However, Professor Simon Burgess who processed the data, said it showed that segregation in schools was flat or even declining in some areas.

"We know that people who live in closed communities are more fearful of others and more likely to be prejudiced to people from other backgrounds," added Cantle. He said that anti-extremism measures, including the anti-radicalisation scheme 'Prevent', had "overwhelmed the work on cohesion" since 2007.

Cantle particularly criticised the Coalition Government after 2010, claiming that they removed a duty on schools to promote cohesion and said in a report that "the Government will act only exceptionally" over the issue. "I understand why anti-extremism measures were taken but they were wrong to squeeze out cohesion measures," he said, arguing that the ongoing Casey review was a sign that the government knew it had got the agenda wrong.

It comes as Labour prepares to call for legislation on counter-extremism unveiled in the Queen's speech to be put on hold until there has been a cross-party review of the Prevent strategy.

The shadow home secretary, Andy Burnham, will use the Commons debate on the home affairs legislation to argue that the approach could cause further alienation. He will say: "I believe the Government is getting its approach to tackling extremism drastically wrong.

"It is perceived as highly discriminatory and has created a deep sense of despondency in the Muslim community. Far from tackling extremism, it risks creating the conditions for it to flourish. This goes way beyond party politics and is now a very real issue about the cohesion of our society."

A Home Office spokesman said that Prevent had safeguarded people who might be targeted by terrorist recruiters.

He said it was vital work because the terror threat was real, but argued that it was not targeted at Muslims who were often the victims of extremists. "The Counter-Extremism Strategy is about confronting extremist ideology head-on, supporting mainstream voices, and building stronger and more cohesive communities," he said.

12 May 2016

⇨ The above information is reprinted with kind permission from *The Guardian*. Please visit www.theguardian.com for further information.

Anti-social media: 10,000 racial slurs a day on Twitter, finds Demos

A groundbreaking study by the think tank Demos has found that 10,000 tweets containing a racial slur are posted on Twitter every day.

Researchers revealed the most common racial slurs used on the micro-blogging site included: "p**i", "whitey" and "pikey".

However, as many as 70% of tweets using such language were deemed to be using slurs in non-derogatory fashion – often to describe themselves or their own community – sparking debate about the extent to which Twitter truly is a platform for racism and abusive language.

A total of 126,975 English-language tweets from across the globe were analysed over a nine-day period by CASM, Demos' social media research unit, as part of the project.

Analysis suggests only 1% of tweets used a racial slur in an ideological context within a political statement or in a call to action in the real world. Further analysis found that as few as 500 tweets a day were directed at an individual and appeared on first sight to be abusive.

You are what you tweet

The *Anti-Social Media* report estimates between 50–70% of tweets were used to express in-group solidarity with "re-claimed" slurs used within ethnic groups. It cites "P**i" as one term becoming appropriated by users identifying themselves of Pakistani descent.

Last year also saw much debate over use of the term 'Yid army' by supporters of Tottenham Hotspur, a football club with a strong historical connection to London's Jewish community, to describe themselves.

This research comes as Twitter is being increasingly criticised as a platform for racism. High-profile cases such as that involving ex-footballer Stan Collymore and journalist and feminist Caroline Criado-Perez have led to the introduction and sustained support of a 'report abuse' button on the website.

In December, Labour MP Jack Dromey also caused uproar by referring to his postman as "Pikey" in a tweet. Dromey responded to criticism by explaining that the nickname derived from Corporal Pike, a character in TV show *Dad's Army*, demonstrating the potential for racial slurs deemed offensive to be intended non-offensively.

Jamie Bartlett, Director of CASM at Demos and author of the report, said:

"Twitter provides us with a remarkable window into how people talk, argue, debate and discuss issues of the day.

"While there are a lot of racial slurs being used on Twitter, the overwhelming majority of them are not used in an obviously prejudicial or hateful way.

"This study shows just how difficult it is to know what people really mean on the basis of a tweet. Context is king, and often it's more or less lost on Twitter.'

7 February 2014

⇨ The above information is reprinted with kind permission from Demos. Please visit www.demos.co.uk for further information.

I was escorted off a flight due to racist profiling. Britain must banish this bigotry

Last week, I was demonised and detained after other passengers' baseless claims. Pointing the finger at any woman in a headscarf is no way to tackle extremism.

By Maryam Dharas

"Do you speak English?" has got to be the one of the most patronising questions you can be asked. I'm only ever asked that because I wear hijab, as if being a part of western culture and being Muslim are mutually exclusive. Never mind the fact that I was born and raised in London or that I'm going to a Russell Group university to study English – it seems that I will always be stereotyped and judged first by the scarf on my head.

"Islamophobia has now become racialised. It was my sister and I who were labelled as Isis supporters, with my green-eyed brother, who could pass as white, only being questioned by association"

It was also the first question I was asked as I was escorted off an easyJet plane with my sister and brother at 6am last Wednesday morning at Stansted airport. We'd passed security and boarded the flight to Naples, but just as I was about to nod off we were told there was a seating issue and that all three of us would have to follow the air stewardess, who offered no explanation of where we were going. At the top of the stairs leading down to the tarmac there was a sight I'm not likely to forget in a hurry – a mob of armed police and men in suits waiting for us to meet them.

They informed us that a concerned passenger on our flight claimed my sister and I were reading Isis material on our phones in Arabic, with the words "Praise be to God" visible. We vehemently denied all claims. Arabic? There was no Arabic anywhere on our phones. Our family is of Indian origin – none of us even know how to speak Arabic. They then asked why my sister's passport showed a stamp from Iraq. Ironically, she had gone there to raise money for victims of Isis.

I showed them the timestamps of my WhatsApp conversations to demonstrate how the only thing I had done on my phone that morning was send a message to my dad about how Jeremy Corbyn's policies compare to other leftwing leaders. Unless being a lefty is a crime these days, I had committed no offence. We had been humiliated, demonised and our holiday delayed for nothing.

As Muslims we understand that extremism – coupled with a good dose of fear-mongering – has made people wary, so we take extra precautions at airports so as not to prompt any unwarranted suspicion. I'd ordinarily read a prayer for a safe journey but, being aware of how religion has sadly become synonymous with terror in the eyes of many, I refrained from doing so. My sister had wanted to bring Agatha Christie's *Death on the Nile* to read on the plane but I had scoffed imagining the next day's headline: "MUSLIM WOMAN SEEN BRANDISHING MURDER MANUAL". No chance, especially after I remembered how a woman was recently detained and her reading material, on art and culture in Syria, was treated like it was an Isis handbook.

But despite all that consideration and care we still ended up as targets. It's become apparent that Muslims taking extra care to avoid their behaviour being misconstrued will not stop the bigotry that is rife in our society. Making clear that false accusations are a crime is the first step in tackling the issue of ordinary citizens being vilified, with education to combat ignorance being a close second. If this had happened in any other context, the couple who made the baseless claim against us would be charged with an offence for wasting police time. So why is this prejudice suddenly OK when it's Muslims who are the targets? Is the next step going to be that we're treated as second-class citizens, with the scarf on my head giving people licence to tarnish my name with impunity?

"It seems that I will always be stereotyped and judged first by the scarf on my head"

Islamophobia has now become racialised. It was my sister and I who were labelled as Isis supporters, with my green-eyed brother, who could pass as white, only being questioned by association. There are Sikh men who have been targeted by Islamophobic bigots in the same way Muslims are, simply for covering their heads. The common thread tying the tales of intolerance together seems to be that anyone who doesn't conform to a standardised appearance is made to feel like a criminal. What happened to us and many others is not a mere misunderstanding or mistake, it's racism based on profiling.

Nobody is denying that Islamic extremism is a global issue that needs to be tackled, but pointing an accusing finger at any woman in a headscarf is no way of going about it. The only way for society to progress is for the public to be aware that Muslims are exactly the same as everyone else, and that discrimination and suppressing someone's right to practise their religion without fear of persecution goes against the core democratic values of this country.

25 August 2016

⇨ The above information is reprinted with kind permission from *The Guardian*. Please visit www.theguardian.com for further information.

Teachers said I could be a boxer, but never a mathematician

Role model Dr Nira Chamberlain has it all figured out.

By Poppy Brady

Teachers running a careers day at Dr Nira Chamberlain's school looked at him in disbelief when he told them he would one day like to be a professional mathematician when he grew up.

"No, no," they said. "With your physique you should be a boxer. You'd make a very good one. Look at your jawbone." How misguided they were in yet another example of racial stereotyping.

But Birmingham-born Nira had it all figured out. With a mind far brighter than those trying to push him into a boxing ring, he has made it right to the top of the mathematics world.

He is listed by the Science Council as "one of the UK's top 100 scientists" and last year joined the exclusive list of only 30 UK mathematicians who are featured in the world-famous *Who's Who*, the autobiographical reference book.

He may have been described by Loughborough University as one of the greatest scientific minds, but Nira's feet remain firmly on the ground and he explains mathematics as if he was talking about the football team he supports.

In fact, one of his favourite sayings is a quote from David Hilbert, one of the most influential mathematicians of the 19th and early 20th century. Nira backs Hilbert when he says: "A mathematical theory is not considered complete until you have made it so clear that you can explain it to the first man who you meet on the street."

"I love that," laughs Nira, who is a Fellow of the Institute of Mathematics and its Applications (IMA). "I also like what British mathematician Sir John Kingman once said that 'mathematicians are better if they stay a bit childish and play the game as a game'. This is the key to teaching maths.

"It's not to flood people with practical problems, but to say that this is the best game ever invented. It beats Monopoly, it beats chess and it can help you to land rockets on the moon. The real mathematical advances have been made by people who simply loved maths."

Rather than living in a cloistered academic world, Nira currently works for the company Babcock International Group as a principal consultant for data science and mathematical modelling.

In his day-to-day work he writes mathematical algorithms that solve complex industrial and engineering problems.

And with his abundant enthusiasm, it's clear there is nothing Nira likes more than tackling a mathematical problem for the first time. As he says it himself: "The harder the battle, the sweeter the victory."

He says: "People have to understand that maths is one of the most creative subjects out there. It's the poetry of logical ideas. It seems such a shame that so many people become afraid of maths early on and never shake that off."

Boxing clever with mathematical problems is the nearest he ever got to a boxing ring, despite Muhammad Ali being his lifelong super hero.

Nira's passion is clearly helping the next generation to find maths as exciting as he does. He's the author of a paper about doing long multiplication and percentages without a calculator.

"I worked this out while teaching some inner-city youngsters at a Birmingham Saturday school," Nira told *The Voice*. "They were only about 18 months away from doing their GCSEs and I was horrified when they told me they didn't know how to do long multiplication, so I devised a system for them that was relatively easy."

"Well, you will never be a mathematician, but you could become a singer"

Nira's passion for passing on the baton continues. He was invited by ITV political editor Robert Peston to join the charity Speakers for Schools, which provides state schools with free talks from leading UK figures to inspire the next generation.

This summer he is back in London teaching at the International Youth Science Forum, which attracts 500 of the world's leading young scientists from more than 65 countries.

Now living in Kings Norton, Birmingham, Nira has worked all over the world helping to solve complex industrial problems in France, The Netherlands, Germany and Israel.

But there is one issue that does bother him – and it stems back to when he was a boy at school.

He said: "When one of my sons, who is now a teenager, was about four his infant school teacher asked him what he would like to be. He said he would like to be a mathematician.

"The teacher told him: 'Well, you will never be a mathematician, but you could become a singer.'

"That saddens me. Have we learned nothing down the generations? It makes me angry that so many careers are still being denied. As I always say 'you don't need anybody's permission to be a great mathematician'."

21 August 2016

⇨ The above information is reprinted with kind permission from *The Voice*. Please visit www.voice-online.co.uk for further information.

Post-Brexit racist and religious hate crimes spiked in month after vote

It's been called "celebratory racism".

By Louise Ridley

Race or religious hate crime jumped by more than two fifths in the wake of the EU referendum, official figures show.

The number of racially and religiously aggravated alleged offences recorded by police in July was 41% higher than in the same month last year, the Press Association reported.

It comes after a spike in reported incidents following the poll raised fears of a wave of xenophobic and racist abuse.

A Home Office report also showed that in 2015/16 the overall number of hate crimes logged by forces in England and Wales increased by 19%, with 62,518 offences recorded – a rate of around 170 every day.

In the wake of the EU Referendum result, the Huffington Post UK compiled a list of racist incidents reported on social media.

More than 300 hate crime incidents were reported to a national online portal in the week following the vote – compared to a weekly average of 63, figures from the National Police Chiefs' Council showed.

Since it was published, such stories have continued to emerge.

One expert told HuffPost UK this was a surge in "celebratory racism" because some white Brits felt they have "finally got something" after the referendum.

The result has encouraged a new kind of hostility towards "anyone who is different", as the idea of 'Englishness' becomes exclusively white and Christian, according to Dr Paul Bagguley, from the Centre of Ethnicity and Racism Studies at Leeds University.

Bagguley claimed the leadership crisis in both the Conservative and Labour parties had added to a feeling of lawlessness in which people do things they "frankly wouldn't do" normally.

But expressions of hate have been countered by gestures of solidarity. From flowers being handed out at school to dozens of cards being sent to a Polish centre that was the target of racist abuse people have been going out of their way to make sure people of other cultures feel welcome.

"Love and solidarity" protests took place in July at London Tube stations, where people held flowers and messages of peace, and gave out stickers, love hearts and information on how to report hate crime.

13 October 2016

⇨ The above information is reprinted with kind permission from The Huffington Post UK. Please visit www.huffingtonpost.co.uk for further information.

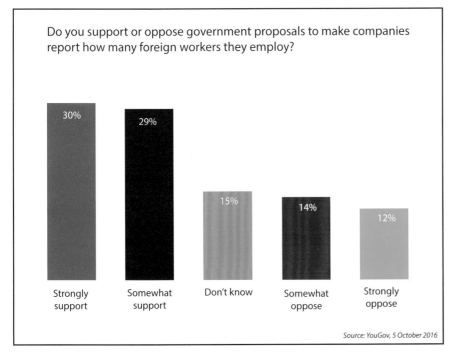

Do you support or oppose government proposals to make companies report how many foreign workers they employ?

- Strongly support: 30%
- Somewhat support: 29%
- Don't know: 15%
- Somewhat oppose: 14%
- Strongly oppose: 12%

Source: YouGov, 5 October 2016

To not see race is the most privileged thing of all

By Amit Singh

A year-old video started circulating on my Facebook page recently in which Nigel Farage declared that Britain needed to scrap its anti-discrimination laws because people are now "colour-blind" and thus cannot be racially discriminative.

With this statement Farage is perpetuating the commonly touted myth in our post-colonial society that nowadays, in the aftermath of various race riots and discriminatory laws, including Jim Crow in America, racism no longer exists – people just see other people.

"If you claim to not see race you are suggesting that a disproportionate number of BAME people are in prison across Europe and America because they are naturally more prone to violence, or that there are an overwhelming lack of high profile people of colour in almost all positions of power because of a serious lack of talent"

This view is very popular amongst certain sections of society – just look at the #AllLivesMatter response to the #BlackLivesMatter movement – who cannot fathom the idea of racism and who do not want to confront their own racial prejudices.

Do you remember the shock and horror of award winning singer Sam Smith when he discovered earlier in the year that racism still existed?

Despite centuries of racism in the UK, racism that was exported elsewhere and racism that still thrives today, Smith was outraged upon learning that we don't live in a colour blind society.

People of colour would not have been so speechless after hearing about racial abuse taking place within London (even if it is as multicultural as we're often told).

But by ignoring race and claiming to be colour blind you erase the experiences of those who have lived with – and continue to struggle against – institutional, structural and verbal racism.

If you claim to not see race you are suggesting that a disproportionate number of BAME people are in prison across Europe and America because they are naturally more prone to violence, or that there are an overwhelming lack of high profile people of colour in almost all positions of power because of a serious lack of talent only (even if you

naively point to Barack Obama or Sadiq Khan as examples – these are the exceptions not the rule and both men have suffered serious racial abuse).

These arguments though, smack of privilege for people of colour are not fortunate enough to pick and choose whether they see race or not as it is their lived experience.

Your inability to see anything but fellow humans doesn't mean race hasn't been constructed and doesn't mean that others don't continuously remind people of colour of their otherness.

When a teacher said to me at school "you look like you know when Ramadam is" it wasn't because of anything other than my brown skin.

You may not see race but people of colour see it all the time when they're being locked up, racially abused, assaulted or even as victims of microaggressions such as being stared at on public transport.

People of colour are denied jobs, denied the right to their own culture, all because of the colour of their skin; it's not as easy for them to just stop seeing it.

To say you don't see colour ignores all of this and ignores the privilege inherent with being born in what is very much a white world (even though it is not a choice).

It is also a very convenient way to remove yourself of any guilt or agency in the protection of white supremacy that impacts many people of colour around the world.

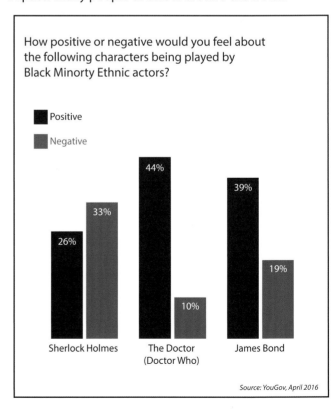

How positive or negative would you feel about the following characters being played by Black Minorty Ethnic actors?

- Positive
- Negative

Sherlock Holmes: 26%, 33%
The Doctor (Doctor Who): 44%, 10%
James Bond: 39%, 19%

Source: YouGov, April 2016

The idea of post-racial society glosses over the structural racism that runs so deep within all societies – it makes us believe that any oppression suffered by people of colour has absolutely nothing to do with their race.

Now that seems like a convenient and effective way to allow racially oppressive structures to continue to exist and thrive.

Race is a total social construct, one constructed in Europe during the time of the colonial civilising missions when people were categorised into racial hierarchies with black at the bottom and white at the top.

Any conversation about race must contextualise this and accept that modern day racism is inseparable from the colonial period and was about more than the colour of people's skin, it was about the cultural supremacy of white Europe over everybody else.

So it's possible to not see race if your friends are highly assimilated into western culture, but that doesn't mean you're not racist, it just means you see them as being nearly white.

You could, for instance, have many BAME friends whilst maintaining a negative view of South Asian or West Indian culture, because you deem them to be alien and inferior to your own.

To refuse to see this ignores the context of how modern racism came to be what it is and ignores the barbaric, violent history of Europe and America

that put these regions in a position to claim to be superior to those elsewhere.

Any notion of being race blind is nothing more than racist ignorance that protects and accelerates the status quo.

The reason people can afford not to see race is because they are white, they are comfortable and they aren't constantly reminded that they are different.

They are able to see through the racial constructions because these do not impact upon them and they have so much privilege that they can choose to ignore it.

People of colour who are systematically oppressed cannot pick and choose whether they see race or not – they see it every day and cannot unsee it, because that is their experience.

If you are someone that speaks of how "colour-blind" they are then perhaps consider all of that and consider what a fortunate position you are in if you can choose to see past these social constructs that are our racial classifications.

21 June 2016

⇨ The above information is reprinted with kind permission from Consented. Please visit www.consented.co.uk for further information.

© Consented 2017

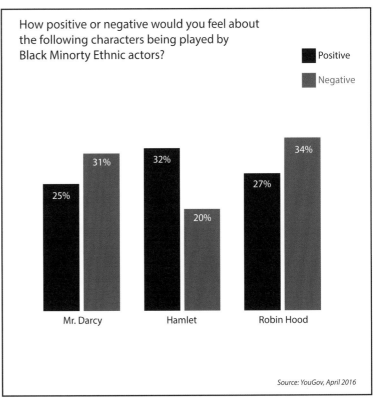

How positive or negative would you feel about the following characters being played by Black Minorty Ethnic actors?

■ Positive
■ Negative

Mr. Darcy: 25% / 31%
Hamlet: 32% / 20%
Robin Hood: 27% / 34%

Source: YouGov, April 2016

Six things I wish people understood about being biracial

By Jenée Desmond-Harri

According to the results of a DNA test I took recently, my ancestors on my father's side are mostly from West Africa (via Arkansas), and the ones on my mom's side come from Europe. When strangers inquire about my racial background, I tend to try to de-escalate their interest. I say things like, "I'm just your run-of-the-mill mixed person with a white mom and a black dad." In other words: nothing super exotic. Nothing to see here.

Why am I so dismissive? I'm a little self-conscious about engaging in excessive navel-gazing regarding my racial identity. It hasn't been particularly difficult for me to manage. If anything, it may have made life easier for me and meant I've encountered less racism than people who have two parents who identify as black. I definitely don't consider myself a "tragic mulatto."

And with nine million Americans selecting more than one race on the last Census – not to mention a president who has a white mother and a black father – it's hard to argue that being "mixed", "multiracial" or "mulatto" (I've been called all of those) in 2015 is really all that unusual.

But I can't deny that as long as race and racism are hot topics in our culture, biracial and multiracial people will continue to be a source of curiosity and fascination. Confession: even I find myself looking a little longer at mixed-race families on the streets of Washington, DC, craning my head to see which parent the children resemble most and wondering how they'll see themselves. As a writer, I've been amazed by the way articles about interracial couples, families or biracial children intrigue readers every single time. My guess is that it's because these stories provide fodder for people to grapple with the nuances of their own identities and push the limits of racial categories, which is itself sort of fascinating.

So there's nothing wrong with the continued curiosity about the experience of biracial people – whether their parents identify as black and white or some other combination society sees as interesting – but there are a few things I'd like people to know about those of us who are living it.

1) "Blewish", "Blexican", "just human": what we call ourselves is idiosyncratic

Biracial people might call themselves black, white, Asian, Latino, mixed, a "rainbow baby", "just human", a "person of color", "Blewish", "Blexican" or some other label they've concocted that perfectly describes their self-conception. This choice might be a political statement, into which they've put a lot of thought and energy. But it's just as likely to be a simple reflection of what sounds and feels right to them at a particular point in their life, or that it reflects an early internalisation of how other people saw them.

Regardless, the labels we choose aren't about you, and while you're definitely entitled to think of us in whatever way makes sense to you, you don't get a vote when it comes to how we identify. Even if you're one of our parents.

I'm lucky that my mother and father have always understood this. They completely deferred to me, from the time I was a child who shunned racial labels altogether (because I'd picked up on the idea that they were taboo, and I didn't want to stand out as different),

to when in high school I made friends with three other girls who had families just like mine and we — I cringe writing this — called ourselves "Halfricans," to when I went to Howard University, a historically black college, and decided that being biracial was just one way of being black.

I definitely don't consider myself a "tragic mulatto"

I've noticed that some people are much less tolerant. They get tied up in knots when people identify in ways that don't square with their own worldviews or racial maths. Check the comments on any article that refers to Obama as the first black president, and you'll find someone lamenting that he is just as much white as he is black – half and half! – and it doesn't make sense to call him African-American. But he's chosen a descriptor that reflects his life experience, and, hard as it is for some to accept, we don't get to dictate what other people call themselves.

The same deference should be given to those who identify as black and white, or black and Asian, or Asian and Latino, or some other combination, refusing to choose only one label or tick only one box. It's really important to some biracial people that all parts of their heritage are acknowledged equally. That doesn't necessarily mean they're rejecting the parts that jump out at others as the most physically obvious or politically salient. (It also doesn't mean they don't understand that they may face racism based on the way they look, versus the way they feel. It's just that racial identity is a calculation that's more complicated than a simple reaction to prejudice.)

The best bet is to accept that people's labels for themselves reflect only one thing: what's true to them.

2) What we call ourselves might change. Often. It doesn't mean we're confused.

If there's a dominant stereotype associated with biracial and multiracial people, it's that we're confused about who we are. But let's be honest: the very idea of dividing humans into racial categories is confusing. Who's in? Who's out? Where are the borders of each group? Who gets to decide?

When a person whose heritage is more complicated than average adjusts what she calls herself over the course of life, it's not a sign of being racially schizophrenic. It's simply a reflection of the fact that the main handful of racial categories have their limitations and that they can change with time, place and perspective. This malleability may show up in our lives in more obvious ways than it does in the lives of people who know for sure they only check one box, but it doesn't mean we're unstable, unsure of ourselves, or conflicted about who we are.

We might even have different answers when discussing our personal, political, social and cultural identities. This is a perfectly normal and level-headed reaction to a society in which the information people are looking for when they ask "What are you?" might be different depending on whether they're a census-taker, someone in your group of friends, a school or employer gauging interest in affinity groups, your doctor or your hairstylist.

3) We're probably not interested in conducting an impromptu press conference on our identity

This experience isn't unique to biracial or multiracial people. Gay people, very tall people, people with mental and physical disabilities, people who are overweight or have recently lost a lot of weight, people who speak with accents, and pregnant women (just to name a few groups) all have to go out into the world bracing for well-meaning but invasive questions and comments from colleagues and perfect strangers who feel just a little too entitled to having their curiosity satisfied.

This phenomenon is especially striking when it comes to biracial and multiracial people, though. It seems to me that because race is so important in our society, some are very unsettled when they can't place someone immediately.

That's when the questions start coming: what are you? What are your parents? Where are you from? Which of your parents is white? Do you choose one side over the other?

The questions aren't, on their face, offensive – but they're invasive, and, just like any other queries about details of someone's family, feelings or upbringing, they can make for uncomfortable, too-personal small talk for those of us who don't like to be put on the spot.

4) We may or may not be sophisticated about or interested in issues related to race

I happen to be really interested in race, racial identity and racism. This might be the result of what I've learned about these topics from an academic perspective or because I'm so struck by the way ethnicity has coloured the experiences of my friends and family, black and white alike.

I think it's common as biracial people for our experiences and observations, and the way people react to us, to inspire us to think more than the average person about race. We may even think we have a little bit of special insight because of the different cultures in which we're embedded. Obama, for example, seemed to display this when he drew on his experience growing up with a white mother and grandmother in his famous race speech.

Because race is so important in our society, some are unsettled when they can't place someone right away

But this isn't the case for all biracial or multiracial people. In fact, a lot of us were raised by parents whose choice to be in an interracial relationship went hand in hand with the fact that they considered themselves postracial, or colour-blind, or that they thought it was tacky or wrong to pay a lot of attention to race.

For example, a reader emailed me recently to say that when her own mixed-race daughters ask about their complexions, as compared with each others' and those of their friends, she simply says, "God doesn't see color." These children probably won't grow up with any deeper level of racial insight than the average American.

That's why although we provide a lot of fodder for people interested in talking and thinking about the complications of race, there's a decent chance that we were trained to do the opposite, and people who meet us shouldn't assume that we're oracles of racial insight or that we make a hobby out of talking about race relations.

5) There's no one biracial experience

This shouldn't be a surprise, given the nine million-plus Americans who identify with more than one race.

That's not even including the majority of black people in America who have some European ancestry even though they have two parents who identify as black – some of them consider themselves biracial, and some of them don't. Many white people have "hidden" African ancestry, too.

Given the thousands of possible variations in heritage, and the way attitudes toward race can change with geography, culture, and even within individual families, it's futile to try to make generalisations about how our lives look, how we feel or how we make sense of the different parts of our heritage.

6) We don't necessarily see ourselves as messengers of racial harmony

"Soon everyone will look like you!"

"One day we'll all be mixed!"

"Beautiful biracial children will show everyone that love has no colour."

These are all things I've heard over the years from people who are really hopeful about eliminating racism. These people seem to think – not entirely unreasonably,

I guess – that the increasing numbers of biracial and multiracial Americans represent the wave of the future and will be ambassadors for understanding, making it harder for us to judge one another and discriminate against one another based on race.

Despite these hopeful comments, there's no evidence that people like me spark racial healing

But personally, I'm put off by the idea that people who look and identify like those on either side of my family have to be wiped out in order to address racism. Plus, to the extent that this scourge has been addressed in American history, it's taken a lot more than people simply showing up and being racially ambiguous. (Just think: the children who were born to white slave owners and enslaved black women didn't do much to change the minds of people who were prejudiced against African Americans. And Barack Obama's presidency has actually triggered increased racial polarisation in American politics.) So while these hopeful comments about a mixed-race future are well intended, there's no evidence that people like me spark racial healing.

That's not to say the lives of biracial people can't provide any insight into, or spark fascinating conversations, about American culture. They can. But there's more to be gained from paying attention to our experience now than there is from figuring out how we'll be useful in the future.

11 August 2016

⇨ The above information is reprinted with kind permission from Jenee Desmond-Harris, Vox. com and Vox Medim Inc. Please visit www.vox.com for further information. The original article can be viewed at http://www.vox.com/2015/3/11/8182263/biracial-identity.

Woman receives death threats after speaking out against 'racist' skin-bleaching comments

"What goes on in people's heads that makes them think this is okay to say to someone?"

By Natasha Hinde

A woman who fired back at a Tinder match who told her she should use skin-whitening products to look "pretty" says she has received a slew of death threats and racist remarks for speaking out.

"If you have to say 'not trying to be offensive/racist/mean' before you say something, DON'T SAY IT"

Takara Allen, 22, had been on a date with a guy she met on Tinder called Nikolas when he texted her to say: "Just curious but have you ever thought about bleaching your skin? You'd look so pretty if you were whiter!"

Outraged, Allen, who identifies as black, took to Facebook to complain about the comments. She also took the opportunity to speak out about skin-bleaching in general and the ridiculous beauty standards black women are faced with.

But while many were supportive of her and praised her for saying something, she also received an onslaught of abuse.

She wrote on Instagram: "It can be very nerve-wracking and intimidating to speak up about certain things and to take a stand against racism.

"I've ... been receiving quite a large amount of racist messages, death threats (you know who you are) and the typical 'you're not even black' messages which I'm unfortunately used to."

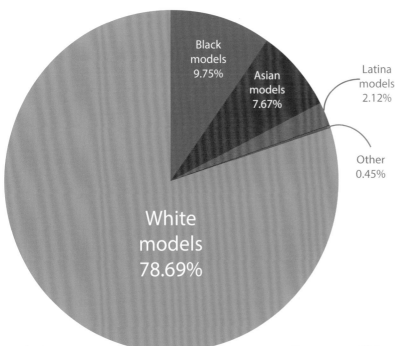

Models of colour at New York Fashion Week
Fall-Winter 2014 Season

Black models 9.75%

Asian models 7.67%

Latina models 2.12%

Other 0.45%

White models 78.69%

Source: Jezebel.com

Allen, who is from Adelaide in Australia, said her Tinder date's skin-whitening comments really upset her.

"Just curious but have you ever thought about bleaching your skin? You'd look so pretty if you were whiter!"

She told the *Daily Mail*: "I was so in shock that someone would ever send that to me that I actually started crying out of frustration. I've never had anyone suggest that I bleach my skin before."

She added: "There's so much pressure for people of colour like myself to conform to European beauty ideals and standards."

After receiving the hurtful message, Allen replied saying: "Have you ever considered drinking bleach because the world would be so much prettier if you did."

The make-up artist also posted an image of their text exchange on Facebook and took the opportunity to speak out about skin bleaching and racism.

She wrote: "What goes on in people's heads that makes them think this is okay to say to someone?

"As if people of colour don't already struggle enough with the pressure to conform to Eurocentric beauty ideals and standards, people like this add even more."

She continued: "I've grown up hearing 'You'd be prettier if you were lighter' and 'You're pretty for a black girl' as if black women are just generally unattractive, and so it's a surprise when one of us is.

"Not to mention the fact that as a mixed race woman people are constantly hitting me with the 'but you're so pretty, what are you mixed with?' bulls*** when I simply say 'I'm black'. As if black can't be beautiful on its own and that I should be grateful to be mixed with something because whatever I'm mixed with makes the black 'okay' all of a sudden."

She added: "People are always complaining that I post too many things talking down about white people ... but none of you realise that this is the s**t that myself and other black women have to deal with on a daily basis.

"It's easy to say 'don't let it get to you' and what not but this isn't a one time thing. I've been hearing this crap ever

since I moved to Australia and I can guarantee you that women who are even darker than I am hear it even more.

"There's so much pressure for people of colour like myself to conform to European beauty ideals and standards"

"If you have to say 'not trying to be offensive/racist/mean' before you say something, DON'T SAY IT."

Since speaking out against the hurtful skin-bleaching comments, Allen said she has received racist messages and even death threats from trolls.

But added that everyone else's "love and support" has outweighed it all.

She said: "I feel like I've done the right thing standing up for myself and I hope at the very least I have helped a few other people gain the confidence to stand up for themselves."

"As a mixed race woman people are constantly hitting me with 'but you're so pretty, what are you mixed with?' [...] as if black can't be beautiful on its own"

As for the guy who sent the hurtful comments in the first place, Tinder has confirmed he's now been removed from the app.

26 April 2016

⇨ The above information is reprinted with kind permission from The Huffington Post UK. Please visit www.huffingtonpost. co.uk for further information.

Racist and sexist assumptions endured in UK media coverage of Malala Yousafzai

A new study has found that seemingly positive media coverage of feminist campaigner Malala Yousafzai is actually full of patronising assumptions about women in Muslim countries.

The study analysed more than 140,000 words of coverage of activist Yousafzai in the nine months after she was attacked by the Pakistani Taleban. It found the fearless and eloquent campaigner was reduced to a passive victim by the British media. In some cases, she was simply referred to as "Shot Pakistani Girl".

The study was carried out by Rosie Walters, a postgraduate researcher at the University of Bristol's School of Sociology, Politics and International Studies. She said: "The West has often been guilty of portraying women in Muslim countries as passive and as victims. Malala Yousafzai challenges that stereotype in every way, which is why I wanted to analyse the coverage of her.

"She even said herself that she doesn't want to be portrayed as the young woman who was shot by the Taleban, but rather as the young woman who bravely fought for her rights. Sadly, the findings of this study show that the British media is far from granting that request."

The research, published in *The British Journal of Politics and International Relations*, used a form of discourse analysis that analyses the words and terms associated with a particular subject (in this case both Malala Yousafzai and her native Pakistan), the assumptions that have to be made for these associations to make sense, and the way in which these assumptions position subjects in relation to one another.

Walters' research found that in more than 140,000 words in *The Daily Mail*, *The Guardian*, *The Independent*, *The Sun* and *The Telegraph*, the word feminist was used just twice, and on neither occasion to refer to Yousafzai, despite her tireless campaigning for the rights of girls and young women. The underlying assumption this demonstrates is that a Pakistani woman cannot be a feminist.

"The coverage positions the UK as inherently superior to Pakistan because it has supposedly already achieved gender equality," said Walters.

"Yet it simultaneously shows that this is far from true. One article even advised Yousafzai on how to dress and behave in her new school in Birmingham so she doesn't come across as too much of a geek. It seems astonishing that a young woman who has come within centimetres of losing her life fighting for her right to an education is being advised to tone down her ambition, in case it makes her seem uncool or unattractive to boys.

"If anything, it suggests that Malala Yousafzai has a great deal she could teach us about fighting to be judged on one's intellect and abilities, and not on gender."

Another interesting contradiction the research identified was in media coverage of Yousafzai's move to the UK, and the medical treatment she received here. While all five newspapers were quick to express pride in the NHS care that she received, they were also keen to emphasise that all her expenses would be met by the Pakistani Government.

In fact, just two weeks after an article in *The Sun* proclaimed: "…the NHS should be proud of its success in treating the brave schoolgirl…", the tabloid published another article with a headline "NHS 'too good to migrants", claiming many doctors were refusing to treat people who weren't British citizens.

Walters said: "The overwhelming outpouring of support and admiration for Malala Yousafzai in the months after the attack represented a real opportunity to re-examine some of the assumptions we make about Muslim women, and also about the kind of people who migrate to the UK in search of safety. Unfortunately, it seems that opportunity was missed."

Although the study focuses on some individual articles to illustrate wider trends, Walters, whose research on girlhood and international politics is funded by the Economic and Social Research Council, was keen to emphasise her study is not a criticism of journalists.

"The point of the study is not about individuals and the vocabulary they use. It's about identifying patterns across many different texts, which tell us a great deal about how we as a nation represent ourselves in journalism, and how we represent other cultures and countries.

"In this case, what it clearly shows is that in our society, it is far easier to label Malala Yousafzai a 'victim' than it is to call her powerful, a survivor, or even a feminist."

19 May 2016

⇨ The above information is reprinted with kind permission from the University of Bristol. Please visit www.bristol.ac.uk for further information.

India's caste system: everything you need to know about the Hindu social hierarchy

By Priyanka Mogul

Although India's caste system dates back centuries, the Hindu social hierarchy has been the source of a number of controversies in the country in recent months. In January, a student from the lowest social class – the 'dalit' – committed suicide, sparking an intense nationwide debate on that group's treatment. In February, violent protests organised by Haryana's 'Jat' community reignited the caste debate as demonstrators demanding job quotas similar to those given to the 'dalit'.

Here IBTimes UK rounds up everything you need to know about the history and current status of the Indian caste system.

The origins of the caste system

Some Hindu theologians believe the India's caste system originated with the Hindu god of Brahma – the creator of the world and all creatures on it in Hindu mythology. It is said that the highest people of society – priests and teachers – were produced from the Brahma's mouth, warriors were produced from his arms, merchants and traders from the God's thighs, and workers and peasants from his feet.

One of the secular theories is that Aryans from central Asia invaded the country and introduced the caste system in an attempt to control India's population by giving each group a different role in society. The roles were based on factors including occupations and diet, as well as perceived qualities such as wisdom and intelligence. In the 20th century this theory was disproved as scholars found that there was no Aryan invasion.

The exact origins and beginnings of the caste system remain difficult to trace; however, the *Manusmriti* – the most important ancient legal text of Hinduism, which British rulers in India used to settle disputes among Hindus relating to inheritance, marriage and royal succession – has cited and justified the caste system in 1000B.C., stating the caste system is a set of "prescribed unequal laws for different castes based upon their status in society" and it "justifies the caste system as the basis of order and regularity of society".

The breakdown of the caste system social groups

The *Manusmriti* recognises five different classes of people within the caste system: the Brahman, Khatriya, Vaishya, Shudra and Dalit.

⇨ Brahman – priests and teachers

⇨ Kshatriya – warriors and rulers

⇨ Vaishya – farmers, traders and merchants

⇨ Shudra – labourers

⇨ Dalit (also known as 'Untouchables') – street sweepers, cleaners

Traditionally, rural communities based every aspect of life on the caste system. The upper caste members lived separately from the lower caste members and even water wells would not be shared with different caste groups. Marriage outside one's caste was forbidden and, in general, the system brought many privileges for the upper castes, while the lower castes suffered repression and discrimination.

Hindus are born into their caste and without the opportunity to marry

into a different social group, people are confined to their caste group for life. This meant that there was no scope for aspiring to climb the social hierarchy ladder and those in the lower castes remained where there were, stalling economic progress. Dalits faced the worst discrimination, with a United Nations report in 2005 indicating that there were more than 31,000 violent acts committed against the 'Untouchables' in a single year.

"In January 2016 a Dalit researcher at the University of Hyderabad committed suicide, sparking a debate on the treatment of the lowest caste members"

Demolition of the caste system

Following the end of British rule in India, the Indian constitution banned discrimination on the basis of caste. In 1950, authorities also announced quotas in government jobs and educational institutions for those lowest in the caste hierarchy. The Government divided the lower castes into 'Scheduled Castes' and 'Scheduled Tribes'. The slightly higher-ranking castes were classified as 'Other Backward Classes' (OBC) and were awarded government quotas in 1989.

The person who authored the Indian Constitution – BR Ambedkar – was a Dalit himself and the occasion marked a significant moment for the country. Ambedkar abandoned his Hindu faith and converted to Buddhism in protest over the way that Dalits were being treated. Mahatma Gandhi also campaigned heavily for the abolition of the caste system. It was Gandhi who renamed the 'Untouchables', 'Harijan' – the people of God.

Today, particularly in urban areas, the influence of the Hindu caste system has greatly declined. Intercaste marriages have become more common; however, family names are often a strong indication of what caste a person belongs to and continues to create a strong sense of identity.

Recent caste-related controversies

Dalit student from 'untouchable' caste commits suicide

In January 2016 a Dalit researcher at the University of Hyderabad committed suicide, sparking a debate on the treatment of the lowest caste members. Rohit Vemula and four of his Dalit friends were reportedly suspended by the university administration days earlier, being told that they could attend classes but were not allowed to enter the hostel or common areas. Being unable to afford private housing, the Dalit group set up camp in front of the university and began a hunger strike in protest against their "social boycott".

Haryana Jat reservation protest

In recent years, a number of communities have been demanding the right to be recognised as OBCs. The most recent was the Jat community protests in Haryana in February 2016. At least 18 people were killed after the protests turned violent, while protesters cut off a key water supply to Delhi, leaving much of the capital without water for days. The issue caused controversy among the general public as the Jat community is regarded as a prosperous and politically dominant community. However, Jat leaders insisted that they should be granted government quotas as they claim that large numbers of their communities are poor.

27 February 2016

⇨ The above information is reprinted with kind permission from the *International Business Times*. Please visit www.ibtimes.co.uk for further information.

© *International Business Times 2017*

Race at Work

Executive summary from the Business in the Community report.

The voices of 24,457 individuals cannot be ignored

This *Race at Work* report provides us with greater understanding of the issues around this under-representation of ethnic minorities in the workplace and at senior levels. In this report we share the experiences of 24,457 ethnic minority and white employees aged 16 and over and currently in employment in the UK (England, Wales, Scotland and Northern Ireland). The participants took the race at work survey via a YouGov panel survey (6,076 respondents) and a public open survey (18,381 respondents).

In the UK today, Black, Asian and Minority Ethnic (BAME) people are under-represented at every management level in the workplace. One in eight of the working age population is from a BAME background, yet only one in ten are in the workplace and only one in 16 top management positions are held by an ethnic minority person.[1] British people with a BAME background are more likely to enjoy their work but are less likely to be rated as top performers compared to their white counterparts.[2]

BAME people are more likely to enjoy their work and have far greater ambition than their white colleagues. 64% of BAME and 41% of white employees in the panel survey said it is important that they progress. This is amplified in the open survey with 84% of BAME employees and 63% of white employees saying it is important to progress.

⇨ Racial harassment and bullying within the workplace is prevalent. 30% of those employees who have witnessed or experienced racial harassment or bullying from managers, colleagues, customers or suppliers report it has occurred in the past year alone.

⇨ Many UK employees do not feel valued or inspired. Many employees do not have access to career role models, nor are they inspired, feel supported or valued by their managers. This is felt most keenly by people from an ethnic minority background; BAME employees are less satisfied with their experiences of management and progression than white employees and just over half of the open survey respondents feel that they are working as part of a team. The lack of role models in the workplace is particularly stark for Black Caribbean (11%) and Other Black group (7%) employees, with Chinese and Mixed race employees lacking role models both inside and outside of the workplace.

⇨ We are not comfortable talking about race at work. UK workplaces might be comfortable talking about age and gender, but are less comfortable talking about race. It is clear employers need to have more confidence to address the issue of race at work and aim to understand how it has an impact on the individual and their opportunity to reach their full potential.

⇨ Getting on the fast-track is an unequal business. Interest in taking part in a fast track programme is significantly higher among BAME groups, jumping from 18% of white employees who would take part to 40% of BAME employees. However, this is not reflected by greater access to fast track management programmes or inclusion in succession planning for all ethnic minority groups. The leadership pipeline of today needs to be populated with sufficient BAME talent to ensure that senior management of the future reflects an increasingly diverse working age population.

There is some good news

There is some evidence that workplaces are responding to a high demand for mentors from BAME employees. Access to a sponsor is important when any group is under-represented at senior levels and there is some evidence that BAME people are more likely to have access to a sponsor than white employees. Where these relationships exist, BAME people respond positively – they feel valued and actively supported in their career progression.

5 November 2016

⇨ The above information is reprinted with kind permisison from Business in the Community. Please visit http://workplace.bitc.org.uk for further information.

© Business in the Community 2016

1 *Race at the Top*, Business in the Community, June 2014

2 *Gender and Race Benchmark 2014: Performance and Appraisal*, Business in the Community, 2014

Teaching profession fails to reflect multi-cultural student population

There is a severe shortage of ethnic minority professionals at every level of education, charity finds.

By Kate Hodge and Sarah Marsh

Ethnic minority professionals are under-represented at every level of education, according to a new report from youth employment charity Elevation Networks.

The report, which analysed research on employment in UK state-funded primary and secondary schools, found that last year just 6% of state primary school teachers and 9.9% of qualified and unqualified teachers in maintained secondary schools were from black, Asian and minority ethnic (BAME) backgrounds.

The research also analysed colleges, universities and higher education, where the picture was equally disappointing: just 7% professors and 8% of senior lecturers were from BAME backgrounds.

This compares unfavourably with the UK population overall as a whole as the last UK census in 2011 showed that 13% of people identified as BAME. This percentage is even more pronounced in schools: 30.4% of primary students and 26.6% of secondary students in state schools are from minority ethnic groups, according to figures from the Department for Education (DfE).

The research, *Race to the Top: 2*, also highlights a long-standing lack of diversity in senior leadership in schools: just 3% of headteachers in state-funded primary schools and 3.6% in maintained secondary schools are from an ethnic minority groups.

Nicole Haynes, a headteacher at Mount Carmel Catholic College for Girls, says the gap at senior and middle leadership level is disappointing. She puts this in part down to the recruitment process, saying interview panels are often not ethnically or gender-balanced.

Mary Bousted, general secretary of the Association of Teachers and Lecturers, agrees: "It's absolutely the case that ethnic minority teachers are unrepresented in the teaching profession, but more so in school leadership roles and that's worrying in a multicultural society because children need to see teachers and school leaders from BAME role models to show the importance of education."

A comparison of teacher workforce research with census data suggests there's an over-representation of BAME teachers in outer London and the south-east. The West Midlands, however, suffers the worst shortfall: 6,613 ethnic minority teachers would be needed to ensure staff represent their student populations.

As well as affecting student engagement with school, the lack of role models could also deepen the staff recruitment and retention crisis that plagues teaching. Commenting on the report, Christine Blower, general-secretary of the National Union of Teachers, said: "It is very important that the teaching profession, alongside all other professions, is representative of modern British society. The prejudice and barriers that BAME communities face mean that many do not consider teaching as a profession despite the important role they could play."

Based on current figures, the report estimates that we would need 51,132 more primary school teachers and 14,429 more secondary teachers to achieve proportional representation.

But these do not seem to be forthcoming. According to 2013–14 statistics from the National College for Teaching and Leadership, just 12% of trainee teachers were from minority ethnic groups – a figure that has remained fairly consistent for five years.

Bousted suggests schools-based teacher-training has exacerbated the pipeline problem for recruiting minority ethnic teachers. She said: "Ethnic minority candidates are less likely to get accepted into these training programmes because of bias. It might not be conscious but we know that school-based training [programmes] accept fewer BAME teachers and one of the reasons for this is that when universities co-ordinated teacher training there were lots of ways they supported applications for ethnic minority candidates, such as through access courses."

The report makes a number of policy recommendations to improve diversity among education professionals, such as having more work experience/volunteering opportunities that feed into the teacher-training programmes. It also suggests making the curriculum more representative to encourage BAME students to consider teaching as a career.

Dr Debbie Weekes-Bernard, head of research at the Runnymede Trust, says research supports this recommendation. She said: "Where minority ethnic pupils have a negative experience of education they are less likely to consider teaching as a potential future career. A great deal of work explores the very low numbers of particularly black students choosing history as a degree subject [and how this] has had an impact not just on those taking initial teacher training courses featuring history as a specialism but also on those going on to study and then teach it as a subject within universities."

19 November 2015

⇨ The above information is reprinted with kind permission from *The Guardian*. Please visit www.theguardian.com for further information.

What to do if you're worried about racism

Following the EU referendum, you may be worried about reports of an increase in race hate incidents, in particular towards migrant workers and ethnic minorities. In addition, if you are an EU national working in the UK, you may feel uncertain about your future position.

Below is some useful information about your rights, what you can expect, and where to go for help and support if you experience racism at work or elsewhere.

Your rights at work

All employees have the right to:

⇨ Work in safe and healthy conditions

⇨ Not be threatened, harassed or bullied

⇨ Not be discriminated against

⇨ Complain about poor treatment without being victimised

EU nationals working in the UK

EU citizens still have the right to live, work or get benefits in the UK. This will not change until the UK stops being a member of the European Union or a new agreement is negotiatied for EU nationals already resident in the UK. That process could take some time, and changes will be announced before they happen, so there is no need to rush to take any action.

Talking about contentious political issues

⇨ Any discussion about contentious political issues should be conducted sensitively and with respect for the views and positions of others.

⇨ We all have the right to freedom of expression, but this does not extend to the protection of speech that discriminates against, harasses or incites violence or hatred against others.

Race hate incidents

There have been reports of an increase in racism and hate incidents. These are criminal offences.

The National Police Chiefs' Council has said that:

"Victims and those feeling vulnerable will receive support from the police and offenders can expect a strong response and enhanced sentencing.

Where to get information and help

⇨ If you have any worries, you can discuss these with your line manager.

⇨ If you are a union member, speak to your union representative.

⇨ If you believe you have been discriminated against, contact the Equality Advisory and Support Service on 0808 800 0082.

⇨ Anyone who experiences a race hate incident can report it by calling the police on 101. In an emergency, always dial 999.

⇨ You can also use True Vision, the official website for reporting hate crime – www.report-it.org.uk. True Vision have information about third party reporting centres for those who do not want to go the police directly. These centres also provide advice and support.

⇨ In Scotland, report hate incidents directly on the Police Scotland website – https://www.scotland.police.uk/secureforms/hate-crime/

⇨ You can also contact the independent charity Crimestoppers anonymously on 0800 555 111.

⇨ If you are an EU national, you can get information relevant to people from your country of origin from your embassy or consulate. If you need help to find your embassy or consulate, please contact Citizens Advice at www.citizensadvice.org.uk or call 03444 111 444.

⇨ Victim Support helplines: England and Wales – 0808 168 911; Scotland – 0345 603 9213.

⇨ For impartial advice on tackling race hate incidents in the workplace, contact Acas (Advisory, Conciliation and Arbitration Service) at http://www.acas.org.uk/index.aspx?articleid=5771.

⇨ The above information is an extract from the publication *What to do if you're worried about racism*. It is reprinted with kind permission from the Equality and Human Rights Commission. Please visit www.equalityhumanrights.com for further information.

⇨ Adapted from https://www.equalityhumanrights.com/sites/default/files/what-to-do-if-youre-worried-about-racism-eu-referendum-factsheet.pdf.

⇨ The copyright in the document this publication has been adapted from and all other intellectual property rights in that material are owned by, or licensed to, the Commission for Equality and Human Rights, known as the Equality and Human Rights Commission ("the EHRC").

© Equality and Human Rights

Race relations after 50 years

By Sir Geoffrey Bindman QC

This year marks the 50th anniversary of the statute which originated equality legislation in Britain: the Race Relations Act 1965. In the last 50 years, anti-discrimination law has proliferated. The Equality Act 2010 consolidated laws which now extend to eight protected characteristics: age, disability, gender reassignment, marriage and civil partnership, race, religion or belief, sex and sexuality. The act of 2010 combines the effect of nine statutes and over 100 statutory instruments.

Few would now question the role of the law in promoting equal treatment. Yet the original statute was novel not only in its subject matter but also its approach to enforcement, which had no earlier parallel in Britain. The Labour Government which introduced the Race Relations Bill in 1964 had initially provided for criminal penalties on those found guilty of what was to be the crime of racial discrimination. After the Bill was introduced in the House of Commons, however, Roy Jenkins became Home Secretary. He was receptive to a different approach, putting conciliation rather than punishment in the forefront, and with civil rather than criminal sanctions if conciliation could not be achieved.

This approach had been adopted in the USA. In Britain the Campaign Against Racial Discrimination (CARD) and a sub-committee of the Society of Labour Lawyers had examined the long history of anti-discrimination strategies in that country. After the anti-slavery states of the north won the civil war in the 1860s, legislation was introduced to criminalise not only slavery itself but a wider range of discriminatory treatment based on supposed racial difference. But criminal sanctions did not work: white juries declined to convict other white people for conduct which they regarded as justified.

So the law against discrimination became a dead letter and remained so for nearly a century. After 1945, a few US states, such as New York and Massachusetts, established administrative agencies to investigate complaints of discrimination. Their primary aim was conciliation, but they could seek judicial sanctions against perpetrators who failed to provide adequate redress or take action to eliminate discriminatory practices.

Roy Jenkins accepted this model for Britain, but with narrow scope and weak sanctions. The Act empowered a new Race Relations Board to investigate complaints through a network of voluntary 'conciliation committees', but the prohibition of discrimination on grounds of 'colour, race or ethnic or national origins' was restricted to 'places of public resort' – hotels, pubs, libraries, public transport and the like. Timidity and compromise with fierce political opposition denied its application to employment and housing, where discrimination was much more widespread and damaging. Enforcement was weak to the point of non-existent. If conciliation failed, the Race Relations Board's only power was to refer the matter to the Attorney General, who could do no more than seek a County Court injunction to restrain future discrimination. In the life of the 1965 Act not a single injunction was even sought, let alone granted.

The one saving grace of the 1965 Act was a requirement on the board to monitor the effect of the new law and report its findings to the Home Secretary. To assist in this task, two reports were commissioned.

One was a practical survey of the experience of minorities seeking employment, housing and other services carried out by PEP (Political and Economic Planning). Three researchers, one native white British, one white of Eastern European origin, and one black from the Caribbean, applied for advertised vacancies claiming equivalent qualifications. The results were recorded and tabulated, demonstrating massively higher rejection rates for the black applicant and higher rejection rates for the non-native white applicant.

The other report was by a committee of three lawyers under the chairmanship of Professor Harry Street of Manchester University. Geoffrey Howe QC (later Lord Howe of Aberavon) and I were the other members. Our main recommendations were predictable: to extend the scope of the law to employment, housing and other services, and to strengthen enforcement powers.

These recommendations were broadly accepted and enacted in the Race Relations Act 1968. The scope of the law was duly extended. The conciliation system was retained, but if conciliation failed the board was empowered to seek redress in the County Court. This could include awards of damages as well as injunctions to restrain future discrimination.

Over the next eight years the board brought a number of County Court cases, mostly successful but with trivial awards of damages as low as £5. Several of the cases led to protracted litigation with companies and public authorities who were unwilling to accept adverse findings. Yet the legislation continued to have serious weaknesses.

The absence of effective enforcement encouraged the committees to accept virtually meaningless gestures as amounting to conciliation. In some cases they accepted such feeble wording as "we deny having discriminated and we promise not to do so in the future".

In employment cases the position was even more pathetic. Conciliation had to be carried out not by the board's committees but by "industry machinery" – joint committees of employer and union representatives. There was no enthusiasm for the process among employers or trade union leaders and it had little practical effect. I cannot recall a single meaningful remedy for any victim of employment discrimination under the 1968 Act.

Only after the Sex Discrimination Act (SDA) reached the statute book in 1975 did the impetus arise for an effective Race Relations Act. The SDA expanded the definition of discrimination to include indirect discrimination, the cumbersome conciliation process was abandoned and individuals were given the right to take their own cases to courts and tribunals. A start was made to impose positive duties on public authorities to act against discrimination. These early efforts to attack discrimination through law remain the basis of our current system.

The legal framework was complicated and in several respects strengthened by the development of European law and by the extension of the prohibition of discrimination to gender, disability, religion and other fields. The creation of new boards and commissions for some of these fields led to pressure to consolidate – hence the Equality Act and the supposedly comprehensive Equality and Human Rights Commission. Sadly, as so often, consolidation means cuts and the withdrawal of necessary powers and resources. The EHRC has been decimated and can no longer pursue the legal paths which lie at the heart of the legislation.

David Cameron recently commented on the fact that "people with white sounding names are nearly twice as likely to get call-backs for jobs than people with ethnic sounding names". Was he aware that this almost exactly repeats the finding of the PEP report of 1967? "I want to end discrimination and finish the fight for real equality in our country today," he went on. If so, he must restore the funding of the EHRC and the ability of victims of discrimination to assert their legal right to equal treatment.

⇨ The above information is reprinted with kind permission from Runnymede. Please visit www.runnymedetrust.org for further information.

Why we need to stop labelling some black people as white

Telling a black person: "you're so white", does more harm than good…

By Michelle Badipe

I'm sure I'm not the only person that's heard this. The snarky comment mumbled under the breath of the Nigerian aunty, the startled statement that escapes the lips of your white classmate. A lot of us have heard those three identity bending words, words that I used to just brush off, but have now got me thinking what exactly does it mean to be black?

The way I behave has always been deemed as white. The way I speak, the food I eat, my mannerisms and my interests. A friend of mine in high school once exclaimed that I was out of touch with my culture and people, because she was talking about basketball and I couldn't follow what she was saying. There seems to be certain archetypes connected to the black identity – we're supposed to know all the words to Kendrick's new album, know how to dance, be able to run fast, talk in ebonics and act a certain way, such that when one of us doesn't fit this mould, it unravels both black and non-black people.

The white and black community react differently to people who do not act stereotypically black. White people see it as something positive; sure it confuses them, but it also makes them feel like they can relax. Tucker Bryant in his spoken word poem "Oreo" states that when a white person says: "you're so white", it's seen as a compliment, they "expect you to wear their words as a medal" because they don't see you as something that makes them uncomfortable. This is dangerous because it suggests that the white identity is the only identity that is allowed to be versatile, if individuals from other races try to break from the stereotypes that have been set in place by a white society, then they are seen as white, just because they are not adhering to a certain mould.

On the other hand, in the black community, when someone expresses interests that are different from what the community enjoys, we tend to bring that person down. It's not always malicious, we sometimes point these differences out by joking about them, but at the end of the day the aim is to make the individual feel uncomfortable. Some of these differences are pointed out as 'acting white.', a pejorative term that suggests that the individual has betrayed their culture in favour of white culture. Victoria Bond in her article said "It's time to abandon the 'acting white' theory once and for all" and states that "black people in all-black communities police their fellow citizens for their productive behaviours." So if someone is acting in a way that is different, especially if it is productive, the community finds it intimidating. Our communities need to create room for people to explore and expand their identity, so when people say that they enjoy Fall Out Boy, love to read Jane Austen and don't mind *Seinfeld* we shouldn't bring them down.

I find it interesting how we seem to measure blackness by behaviour, when that is not what being black is about. Yes, black people are possibly more inclined to like certain things but that is not what makes us black. Rachel Dolezal, a woman who's made headlines by identifying as black, does and says all the right things and yet she is not black. No matter how hard she tries in interviews to place herself as a black person because of her actions, she is not. What unites us as a body and as a people is the challenges and experiences we all face, because of our race. We're human beings with varied thoughts, tastes and emotions, so that means we don't all have to like and do the same thing. Christian M in his book *Black Identity in the 20th Century: Expressions of the U.S and U.K.* Diaspora defines Black as "persons/groups who can claim African heritage around the world". Blackness comes down to experience and heritage, and not necessarily behaviour.

However, behaviour and actions are affected by our environment. Some of us grew up in different areas, surrounded by different people and cultures, and in the end, that's going to affect how we behave. *Dear White People* is one of my favourite films at the moment, because it carefully explores the identity of black millennials and how we're trying to place ourselves in a world that views us a certain way, but also a community that expects certain things from us. The movie explores the lives of four young black people that have grown up in a predominantly white environment, trying to understand who they are, and if their behaviour is connected to their identity. One girl strives to escape the image of being stereotypically black, she wears straight wigs, pines after white guys and laughs uncomfortably at their slightly racist jokes. Another is a crusader blazing her way through campus, screaming against institutional racism. There's also a quiet boy who just likes to write, and doesn't feel the need to be pulled into political issues around his race. The movie accurately brings forward the idea that not only are black millennials trying to understand who they are in this new world, but also how different we all are, and how our different personalities and behaviours does not take away from us being black.

14 June 2016

⇨ The above information is reprinted with kind permission from Black Ballad. Please visit www.blackballad.co.uk for further information.

A female Prime Minister is not enough: Britain needs a representative Parliament too

While Britain welcomes its second female Prime Minister, a new report by a University of Bristol academic has found Westminster remains disproportionately white, male, and elite.

While Britain welcomes its second female Prime Minister, a new report by a University of Bristol academic has found Westminster remains disproportionately white, male and elite.

"A new report by a University of Bristol academic has found Westminster remains disproportionately white, male, and elite"

The Good Parliament report, launched in Parliament today [20 July] by Professor Sarah Childs, shows Parliament's working practices still reflect the traditions and preferences of those who historically populated it.

The report sets out a clear and comprehensive reform agenda. It concludes it is time for Parliament to accept an institutional responsibility to become more representative and inclusive. It makes 43 recommendations, which aim to transform who sits in the House of Commons, significantly enhance MPs' effectiveness, improve the quality of parliamentary outcomes, and ultimately raise the public's regard for the House of Commons.

Professor Childs, from the School of Sociology, Politics and International Studies, was seconded to the House of Commons in September 2015 to work on the report, at the request of the Speaker, the Rt Hon. John Bercow MP.

Professor Childs said: "As we welcome the second female prime minister, we must not forget that Parliament itself remains far from diverse and inclusive. Change will not happen on its own. Parliament needs to accept its responsibility to ensure a diverse composition of MPs and that present members are able to equally participate. Established ways of working need to be questioned."

The Speaker has set up a new group of MPs – 'The Commons Reference Group on Representation and Inclusion' – to lead the reform agenda. It comprises a small number of MPs, male and female, nominated by the parties. Formally chaired by the Speaker, it will meet after the summer recess and will draw up a programme of action for the rest of the Parliament.

Mr Bercow said: "I am delighted to launch Sarah's report, which is the result of a great deal of work and extensive consultation with Members and staff. Not everyone will agree with every recommendation or suggested outcome, which is a condition of an independent report, but I am confident that my colleagues on the Commons Reference Group will scrutinise its contents very closely, with a view to taking on board a good number of its suggestions."

Each of the 43 recommendations is attached to a named, responsible decision-maker, so Parliament and individual members are held to account. The recommendations focus on three elements:

⇨ **Equality of participation.** The report asks how a diverse group of MPs might be selected for, and elected to, Parliament and how, once present, they could be most effective in representing their constituents' interests, scrutinising laws and holding the Government to account. Specific recommendations are made to the new Reference Group, the Secretary of State for Women and Equalities, the House of Commons Commission, the Women and Equalities Committee, and the political parties.

"Parliament is still unrepresentative of the British public, clinging on to antiquated traditions and a reluctance to progress"

⇨ **Parliamentary Infrastructure.** This covers everything from the buildings and furniture of Parliament to the official rules and working practices. Recommendations are made to the Speaker, the House of Commons Commission, the Leader of the House, the Liaison Committee, and IPSA.

⇨ **Commons Culture.** This dimension looks beyond the formal rules to examine Parliamentary culture and its effect on diversity. Recommendations are aimed at the Speaker of the House, The House of Commons Commission, the Women in Parliament All-Party Parliamentary Group (APPG), and the Works of Art Committee.

MPs and academics have lent their support to the report. Tom Brake MP, Liberal Democrat spokesperson for Foreign Affairs, said: "With the creation of the Commons Reference Group on Representation and Inclusion, the political establishment is presented with a real challenge – do we want to ensure Parliament is representative of the UK as a whole or not? And if we do, are we willing to implement the measures necessary to make it happen?"

Dr Meryl Kenny, Lecturer in Gender and Politics at University of Edinburgh, said: "Women are still only 29.4 per cent of the House of Commons, which is simply not good enough. *The Good Parliament* report provides a landmark and much-needed call for change, setting out a comprehensive plan of practical reforms that will fundamentally transform the membership, infrastructure and culture of the House of Commons. The House can – and must – deliver on this new vision of a 'Good Parliament' – one that is modern, representative, accountable and effective. The time is now."

Maria Miller MP, Chair of the Women and Equalities Select Committee, said: "I welcome the recommendation that the Women and Equality Select Committee be made permanent. It is important that the House of Commons takes this report's finding into account when Select Committees are agreed in the usual way after the next General Election.

"The Women and Equality Select Committee has an important role in scrutinising the effectiveness of the Government's equality work. It's important the House of Commons, as a separate body, accepts its institutional responsibility to ensure Parliament is diverse in its composition and more inclusive in its structures and practices.

"As someone who is committed to a fairer and more equal Britain, I look forward to working with the new Commons' Reference Group on Representation and Inclusion."

Melanie Onn, MP for Great Grimsby said: "It is obvious to even the casual observer that Parliament needs to commit to change if it wants to be fit for modern purpose.

"Parliament is still unrepresentative of the British public, clinging on to antiquated traditions and a reluctance to progress. This makes it less appealing as a place to work and causes people to view it as remote and opaque.

"I hope Professor Childs' report will spark the changes we need to see in Westminster."

Dr Eilidh Whiteford MP, Shadow Group Leader on Social Justice, said: "This report makes a really important contribution to the debate about how we make Parliament more representative of those it serves, and how we might work towards better gender balance in our democratic institutions. It deserves to be widely read."

20 July 2016

⇨ The above information is reprinted with kind permission from the University of Bristol. Please visit www.bris.ac.uk for further information.

© University of Bristol 2017

Intolerance in northern Europe

% who have a negative impression of the following groups

	Roma/Gypsies	Muslims	Black people	Gay people	Jewish people
Denmark	72	45	11	7	8
Finland	53	45	20	15	10
France	55	40	14	14	10
Britain	58	40	8	9	7
Germany	42	36	10	12	9
Norway	40	37	11	11	10
Sweden	45	36	8	7	6

Source: YouGov May 2015

We need more than safety pins to stop racism

I have no doubt that the initiative was started with the best of intentions, but sadly it does more harm than good.

By Hussein Kesvani

Yesterday, a close friend was racially abused while taking her normal commuter train home.

A second generation, hijab-wearing Pakistani immigrant, she had been reading a newspaper when two men sat opposite her and taunted her about Brexit. "You better pack your bags and go home" one of them had sneered, while the other had used various expletives, including calling her a "P**i" and a "sand n***er". Despite other passengers being on the train, she was forced to get off at the next stop, and wait another hour to get back home.

Since last week's vote to leave the European Union, the number of similar reported attacks on immigrants and ethnic minorities has surged. According to True Vision, the police hate-crime monitoring website, there's been a 57 per cent increase in reported incidents of abuse since last Thursday. Meanwhile, Tell MAMA, a hate crime monitoring organisation say they've seen a spike in racist attacks on Muslims, adding to a 300 per cent increase in Islamophobic abuse in the past year.

This surge might come as a shock to many. But for most ethnic, religious and sexual minorities (and especially those who make up the intersections) this isn't anything new. In fact, as many have said online in the past week, last week's vote didn't create the racism we're currently seeing. Rather, the overtly racialised, anti-immigrant narrative of both leave campaigns certainly made racism seem acceptable. To put it simply, for many ethnic minorities, the racism that's surging has always existed, and we've had to experience both the subtle and the overt. But it's only now, as those close to us (or at least, those who we have as friends on Facebook) describe instances where they've been racially abused, that swathes of the media and the general public, intent on believing in the existence of a post-racial society, have realised racism has been allowed to fester.

One reaction to this surge has been the 'Safety Pin' initiative – which urging people to wear safety pins as a sign of 'solidarity', an outward message which indicates to ethnic minorities that "you are safe around me". The movement seems to have caught on, as I saw several people on my morning commute donning the pins.

I have no doubt that the initiative was started with the best of intentions, but sadly, I'm not convinced that it's a practical way of helping the most vulnerable feel safe, and in fact, does more to perpetuate some of the worst-informed narratives on race in this country.

For starters, that's because anyone who has experienced racial abuse in public, including myself, are largely aware that not everyone is a racist, as the pin wishes to assure us.

But we're also aware that such messages do little to stop, or limit actual incidents of racism itself – whether that's being followed around a shop by security guards, being discriminated against in a workplace, or being told to "f**k off back home" on a train full of commuters. Feeling safe isn't knowing that someone, somewhere out there is wearing a safety pin because they respect your existence. It's the knowledge that said person is willing to step in when you feel the most powerless, even at the expense of their own safety.

But there's a more problematic side to the Safety Pin campaign too. Ultimately, it reduces racism to overt, visible acts. One that denies legitimate racism as physical action recognisable to white people. Those who partake in the campaign may claim they are doing so to stand in solidarity with those subjected to post-Brexit racism and harassment. But such solidarity means little if the only form of abuse being stood up to is intense, physical abuse without acknowledging the wider settings in which such attacks are permitted in the first place.

That means recognising a larger context of oppression, faced particularly by the poorest and most disenfranchised. The type of abuse that affects such people psychologically, by encouraging them to suppress their emotions, and opinions to justify their existence. And in turn, to diminish the everyday experiences that inform how they live their lives.

Part of the reason why minorities are so much more vulnerable now comes down to the dehumanisation they faced during the bitter referendum battle. But this dehumanisation wasn't caused by any side of the campaign, but rather the forcible silence they faced on all sides of the political spectrum, that ultimately reduced them to their heritage.

As I said on Twitter yesterday, the Safety Pin campaign may be well intentioned, but for many, reads only as a visual symbol for "Not all white people". To truly combat racism in Britain, we need less of these sartorial symbols, and more assurances that the experiences of those who have dealt with and fought racism will be taken seriously.

1 July 2016

⇨ The above information is reprinted with kind permission from *The Independent*. Please visit www.independent.co.uk for further information.

Why we should talk to children about race

An article from The Conversation.

THE CONVERSATION

By Amanda Williams, Lecturer in Psychology of Education, University of Bristol

It's a situation that many parents dread. Encountering a black man in the street for the first time, a white child might loudly ask something like: "Mummy, why does that man have dirty skin?" After cringing, shushing, or offering a distraction, parents may wonder where this kind of question has come from, how to deal with the situation or indeed avoid it in the future.

From a surprisingly early age, children can distinguish between faces from different racial groups. By the time they are three months old, experiments have shown that white, black and Asian infants tend to look longer at faces from their own racial group or familiar racial groups compared to faces from other, less familiar racial groups. By three to four years old, children can consistently and accurately identify others by race. The ability to differentiate between people on the basis of race improves with age, with teenagers and adults automatically and effortlessly categorising others on the basis of skin colour.

Choosing to be colour blind

In many societies there is a widespread belief that individuals should receive the same treatment regardless of their race, ethnicity, gender and ability. Partly in an attempt to appear egalitarian, many adults adopt a 'colour blind' approach to race – avoiding mentioning race under the guise that if one doesn't 'see' race, then one cannot be considered racist. For example, in studies using a photo identification game, white participants asked to identify a particular face from an array of faces are less likely to use race to describe the faces, particularly when paired in the task with a black partner.

The norms enforced by this behaviour have now become so entrenched that adults tend to find situations that force them to talk about race extremely uncomfortable and anxiety-provoking, leading to a complete avoidance of the topic in social interactions.

Even when interacting with their young children, parents avoid race. In one study that observed the way parents read a storybook created to raise issues about race relations and racial prejudice with their four- to five-year-olds, the majority of parents tended not to mention race, despite it being the theme of the book.

But ignoring race does not make it go away. Like adults and older children, young children are aware of race even if no one seems to be talking about it. This may lead young children to ask questions about racial differences, which are sometimes embarrassing and untimely, in order to gain a better understanding of the world around them.

Only after having acquired a better understanding of social norms regarding race, at around ten years old, do children also begin to show colour blind behaviour and avoid using race to identify the target in a photo identification task. Like adults, older children avoid mentioning race even at the expense of how well they might perform in the task at hand.

But taking a colourblind approach to race is not the best way to promote equality and reduce racial prejudice. Studies with white people who avoid talking about race show less friendly behaviour when playing a photo identification task with a black partner compared to a white partner. Like adults, nine- to 12-year-olds also tend to find situations where they have to talk about race uncomfortable, nerve-wracking and unpleasant.

A new approach

But if colour blindness – and the tendency to avoid talking about race – impacts on relationships between diverse people, what approach should we take in order to resolve racial inequalities? The answer lies in embracing and celebrating our racial differences instead of minimising or even altogether ignoring them.

Fully recognising the multiculturalism in our society appears to be a better strategy. For example, in one study children who were read a story that placed value in racial diversity were found to be more likely to identify acts of racial discrimination and more likely to sit next to racially diverse peers in the school lunch room. In another study, white adults who adopted a multicultural approach (as opposed to a colourblind approach) showed less prejudiced behaviour when conversing with an Asian partner about racism and diversity.

Our concerns about discussing race can be reduced by placing more value in racial diversity, resulting in less stressful and more successful interactions with people from racial groups different from our own. As a caveat, most of the research mentioned in this article has focused primarily on the reactions of white participants. So there is more work to do researching attitudes and behaviour in diverse contexts with individuals who identify as racial minority group members.

For children, curiosity about their surroundings and the people they meet comes naturally. Rather than brushing aside children's questions about race in an attempt to avoid social embarrassment, we ought to embrace and celebrate the differences that make us unique, remarkable, and that colour the world we live in.

Talking with children about race from an early age may not only derail embarrassing questions, but may, more importantly, serve to increase children's comfort when interacting with people from different racial and ethnic groups – and increase the comfort of those they are interacting with too.

Given that we live in a society that is becoming increasingly diverse, children will be expected to interact with individuals from many racial and ethnic backgrounds. Children need to be prepared for this future – one way to do this is to encourage them to see this diversity as a positive feature of their worlds. It's time to talk about race.

15 August 2016

⇨ The above information is reprinted with kind permission from *The Conversation*. Please visit www.theconversation.com for further information.

What to do about racist bullying

Britain is a multi-racial and multi-faith country and everyone has the right to have their culture and religion respected by others. Nobody has the right to call your child names or to treat them badly because of their colour, race or religion. It's illegal and it can be stopped. Racist bullying is not just about the colour of your skin, it can be about your ethnic background or religion too. Racist bullying is the only type of bullying that schools must record.

What is racism?

Racism means you are subjected to abuse and harassment because of your race, colour or beliefs. There is a difference between racial discrimination and racism. Racial discrimination means being treated differently to someone else because of your race, perhaps by being told you cannot wear a turban if you are a Sikh, a yarmulka if you are a Jewish boy or hijaab if you are a Pakistani girl.

The complaints we've had include a girl aged six being told by a classmate that she cannot take the school mouse home because he doesn't like people with brown faces, to more serious incidents involving teenage gangs and weapons, one of which meant a boy was too frightened to return to school. These complaints have come from all parts of the UK and are not confined to any particular area.

These complaints have come from all parts of the UK and are not confined to any particular area.

What is racist bullying

In the 1999 MacPherson Report, racist bullying was defined as "any incident which is perceived to be racist by the victim or any other person". Find out more about what anti-bullying policies in schools should cover.

These incidents can include racist abuse, physical threats or attacks, wearing of provocative badges, bringing racist comics or leaflets to school, inciting others to behave in a racist way, racist graffiti and refusing to co-operate with others.

What schools have to do about racist bullying

The Race Relations Act 1976 states that schools and governing bodies have a duty to ensure that students do not face any form of racial discrimination, including attacks and harassment. Read more about anti-bullying policies for schools.

Racism means you are subjected to abuse and harassment because of your race, colour or beliefs or ethnic background. Bullying UK, part of Family Lives, receives many complaints about racist bullying. If you are being bullied in this way you must tell your parents and ask them to write to your head teacher about it. Keep a diary of who says and does what because that will help the school to see where the bullying is taking place.

Your parents need to make a complaint to the police if the school doesn't act to sort out racial bullying.

Making a complaint to the police about racist bullying

You need to make a complaint to the police if the school doesn't sort out racial bullying. Most police forces have school liaison officers who should be able to warn the bullies off. In serious cases you could ask whether your local force has a hate crime unit.

The police have been recording racial incidents separately since 1988 and figures have risen nearly every year since then. This is partly due to an increased willingness to become involved but also because it is now much easier to report racist incidents; in some areas you can report them online.

Schools need to know about tensions in their local communities. This information should be provided by the local police. Disputes within the community sometimes end up in school. Schools must keep a record book of the names of perpetrators of racial problems and are expected to work with the police and other agencies including the youth service and the wider community.

If you think your child has been subjected to racial discrimination then you can ask the Equality and Human Rights Commission for advice on what to do about it. People from every background are covered by the Race Relations Act, there has been a case where an English couple complained of their treatment when they moved to Scotland. The Act applies to all schools and colleges, whether or not they are run by your local council or are private schools. School governors and school boards also have to be mindful of the law which covers admission, how they treat pupils and exclusion as well as decisions on special educational needs.

Racist bullying is an offence

If your child has been threatened or attacked because of his/her race, then you must contact the police. Parents say that the police are generally very helpful and this may be because they are now much more aware of racist issues themselves.

It is now a criminal offence under the Crime and Disorder Act 1998 to racially harass or assault anyone and the Public Order Act 1986 makes it an offence to use threatening, abusive or insulting language or behaviour to stir up racial hatred. Racist leaflets are also outlawed.

Since 2001, amendments to the 1976 Race Relations Act mean that complaints of racial discrimination in education can be brought straight to the county courts (England, Wales and Northern Ireland) or sheriff courts (in Scotland) without having to be referred first to the Secretary of State for Education.

⇨ The above information is reprinted with kind permission from Bullying UK. Please visit www.bullying.co.uk for further information.

© Bullying UK 2017

How apps and other online tools are challenging racist attacks

An article from **The Conversation.**

THE CONVERSATION

By Alana Lentin, Associate Professor in Cultural and Social Analysis, Western Sydney University and Justine Humphry, Lecturer in Cultural and Social Analysis, Western Sydney University

In the aftermath of Brexit in the UK and the success of Pauline Hanson in the Australian Senate elections, racism seems to be a more present threat than ever.

As First Nations people and people of colour in Australia well know, racial violence never went away. But, for others, recent events may serve as a needed reminder that racist attacks and abuses of police power also happen outside the US.

The Brexit fallout has included a sharp rise in racist attacks on people of colour and migrants, including eastern Europeans. Anti-racists in the UK have quickly responded. The iStreetWatch website now allows users to report and map racist incidents across the UK.

People are increasingly using online spaces and digital tools such as anti-racism apps to strategise, challenge racist views and strengthen anti-racist solidarity.

The post-Brexit Twitter handle @PostRefRacism has nearly 10,000 followers. It encourages users "to document the increase in racism in the UK following the vote for Brexit".

But as @PreRefRacism observes, far from being new, racism has merely become more visible to white people since Brexit.

Defining, discussing and countering racism

Activists and scholars have always argued race is a complex formation that needs to be set in historical context. However, the popular view is racism is a matter of bad attitudes that anyone can hold.

In online discussions, reductive approaches to racism can be challenged in real time. It is due to the prominence of many black feminists on Twitter, for example, that the term intersectionality has become more widely understood.

Social media provide an important space in which racism is being defined, discussed and countered. These are key sites for observing how discussions of race take shape.

However, as media scholar Gavan Titley notes, this has also led to racism becoming "debatable" – to the detriment of a clear delineation of what racism is and is not.

While "cyber-racism" is important to challenge, the persistence of street violence and the intertwining of "offline" and "online" worlds call for new methods for opposing racism in public.

Mobile apps for anti-racism interventions and education have been around for a number of years and several more are in development. As our research on apps in Australia, the UK and France has shown, they have diverse functions: to report racist incidents; to educate; and as news sources for racialised communities.

The "phone in your pocket", with its built-in geolocative and image-capturing capabilities, can be a powerful anti-racism tool, enabling immediate reactions to racist events. As with the recent police shooting of Philando Castile, mobile video live-streamed online can generate almost immediate widespread condemnation and reaction.

Tracking Islamophobic abuse

The Australian Islamophobia Watch is a reporting app modelled on one developed by the French anti-Islamophobia association, the CCIF. The app was launched in reaction to the 2014 police raids on Muslim homes and subsequent attacks on Muslim people in public, women in particular.

Like iStreet Watch, the app allows users to report incidents of Islamophobic abuse. A map is created to visualise these incidents by category such as physical

or verbal aggression, discrimination and vandalism. This representation of racial violence is itself a primary purpose of these apps.

The CCIF spokespeople in Paris told us that, in addition to enabling the reporting of racist events, the app-generated data draw attention to the existence of Islamophobia as a category of racism, which is highly contested in France. By cataloguing abusive events, CCIF makes the point that Islamophobia cannot go ignored.

The app includes a feed that provides an alternative news source for an embattled community. Against a backdrop of increased state-sanctioned Islamophobia – bans on hijabs and burqas, the imposition of pork on school canteen menus and heightened policing of Muslims in a hyper-securitised landscape – the resource generates community solidarity.

In this way, users may experience the app as a more concrete response to racism than fleeting online hashtag campaigns.

What are the risks of these apps?

Our research will now turn to the US and Canada where app development has focused on police violence against the black community. Tools such as the NYCLU Stop and Frisk app allow users to film police violence, report incidents and alert users when others are being stopped and frisked in their area.

While such apps purport to put the power in the hands of those on the receiving end, the rise of formalised digital platforms that capture and store data and evidence of racism also raises legitimate concerns:

⇨ As our research shows, the conduit between the reporting

of incidents, the police and the courts necessarily appeals to the same systems in which institutionalised racism so often plays out.

⇨ Despite the apps we studied providing confidential and anonymised reporting, the real and perceived risks of the technology being used (in the wrong hands) to profile and literally locate and track individual reporters and activists is a genuine concern. This may act as a barrier to take-up and use.

⇨ The ease with which incidents can be filmed and uploaded online, while certainly raising awareness, runs the risk of causing people to switch off.

Digital technology can have the dual effect of informing about and banalising racism. As comic Hari Kondabolu tweeted following the US police shootings on successive days of two black men, Alton Sterling and Philando Castile:

"If the cops kill People of Color in the US so easily, even when filmed, can you imagine what our military does in the countries we invade?"

As more apps are developed, more questions will emerge. What is clear is that these will be a main player in the fight against racism as it morphs and spreads into online and mobile-mediated everyday spaces.

13 July 2016

⇨ The above information is reprinted with kind permission from *The Conversation*. Please visit www.theconversation.com for further information.

Employment targets for ethnic minorities will not reduce racial inequalities

Omar Khan, Director of the Runnymede Trust, assesses the prospects for ethnic minorities under the new Conservative Government.

By Omar Khan

The Prime Minister David Cameron's commitments during the 2015 campaign will continue rather than reduce racial inequalities in the labour market. His underwhelming targets suggest we need better evidence, proper legislative scrutiny and public debate to make democracy and fairness a reality for Black and minority ethnic people.

In the final two weeks of the 2015 election campaign, Prime Minister David Cameron gave a speech in Croydon with a message to ethnic minority voters. These included a clear rejection of Lord Tebbit's cricket test (and not simply the easier condemnation of Enoch Powell), as well as the positive message that a Conservative government would support minority faith schools and the benefits of free schools for ethnic minority parents.

In the speech Cameron also referenced employment outcomes. This is hardly surprising, given worse employment outcomes for all Black and minority ethnic groups, and that in the 2010 election unemployment was the single most important issue for BME voters.

A brief scan of the Prime Minister's promises appears positive: a seeming commitment to clearly specified targets, including "20% more apprenticeships". However, on closer inspection, the promises simply commit the Government to the existing underperformance of the apprenticeship policy, and so a further entrenchment of ethnic inequalities in the labour market.

While the Prime Minister positively affirms that 190,000 apprenticeships were taken up by BME people in the last Parliament, that figure represents only 9.5% of the total of two million. Not only were BME people 26% of applicants (and so nearly three times less likely actually to secure an apprenticeship), but race equality organisations and others have been directly asking ministers at the DWP and BIS how they are going to improve these disappointing figures.

On first glance, the "20% more apprenticeships" figure for BME young people looks like a clear recognition of and response to the rise in ethnic inequalities delivered by the apprenticeship policy from 2010 to 2015. However, Cameron's commitment is that BME people will secure 300,000 of the additional three million apprenticeships in the next Parliament, i.e. 2015–2020. This is still only 10% of the total number, meaning that the Prime Minister's target is for BME applicants to be 2.5 times less successful in securing apprenticeships compared to their white British peers. Consider also that 20% of 18- 24-year-olds are BME, or twice the Prime Minster's target, and the much higher rates of unemployment (typically double the white British rate) among BME young people. This suggests that the Government will not seek to reduce racial inequalities even where they are very large and even for 18-years-olds living in Britain today.

The Prime Minister's commitment on employment more generally also initially appears promising: 660,000 more BME people in employment by 2020. This is indeed an impressive-looking figure, and again suggests the Prime Minister is establishing a bold, clear target. However, digging into the numbers, this commitment simply appears to reflect the changing makeup of the working age population over the next five years. Briefly, the older people retiring over the next five years are much less diverse than the younger people joining the labour market over that same period. For example, in the 2011 Census, there were 704,000 BME people aged 20–24, or 20% of the total. Conversely, only 6% of the 3.2 million people aged 60–64 were BME. The commitment to 660,000 more BME people in employment is therefore simply a statement of demographic change in Britain, and appears to require no action from the Government to achieve.

Three points follow from this analysis. First is that the Government has a tendency to quote overall numbers when discussing the labour market, for example the overall number of people in work, or the overall number of BME people getting apprenticeships. They much less frequently cite the various employment rates, or the proportion of people employed, either for the overall population, or for particular demographic groups, whether women or BME people. Because the overall population is growing, as is the BME population (from 5% in 1991 to 14% in 2011 to 30% by 2051), overall figures will always appear positive. Yet if we look instead at employment rates, or the proportion

in work or getting apprenticeships, the figures are far less flattering, and suggest no real improvement in the labour market.

Second is that even if we are generous in interpreting the Prime Minister's commitment as a 'target', it is a very low bar, and one that should easily be cleared, at least in the case of apprenticeships. The third and final point is that the Prime Minister's commitment will result in no improvement – and perhaps a worsening – of ethnic inequalities in Britain. Runnymede and others have questioned before whether policies that benefit all will in fact benefit everyone fairly or equally, but the apprenticeship commitment is in practical terms a commitment to implementing a policy that knowingly and predictably results in less BME people being successful. This not only falls short of an expectation that policies might actually reduce existing inequalities, but it also suggests that government will be unmotivated even to ensure so-called "universal" policies fairly benefit everyone.

In 2012 the Prime Minister rejected the need for equality legislation as so much red tape on the grounds that no government minister or civil servant would ever directly or indirectly design policies that harmed ethnic minorities and other groups. Or, as he put it, "We have smart people in

Whitehall who consider equalities issues while they're making the policy." Previously we might have viewed this claim as benign ignorance of the unconscious and unintended ways in which seemingly fair and universal policies can have unfair and unequal outcomes. With these new 'promises', there are only two conclusions: either the Prime Minister and his aides are unaware of the facts about ethnic minorities in Britain today, or they are unconcerned about the fact that their policies will result in rising ethnic inequalities in the labour market. While briefings about the facts might better inform the clever people in Whitehall and in the Cabinet, proper implementation of the equality duty and greater public mobilisation against racial inequality are the only ways to respond to the latter.

Omar is also a partner of CoDE, the Centre on Dynamics of Ethnicity.

19 June 2015

⇨ The above information is reprinted with kind permission from the University of Manchester. Please visit blog.policy.manchester.ac.uk for further information.

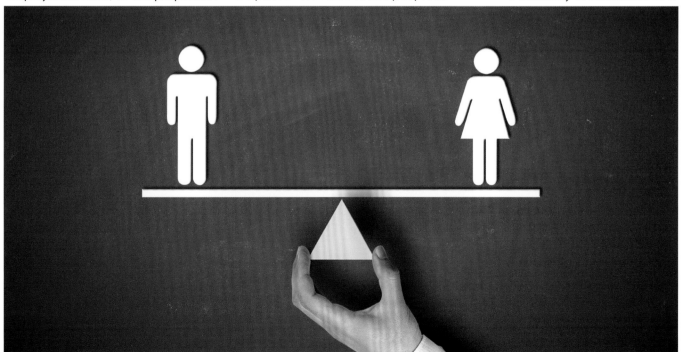

Key facts

⇨ Since 1976 Britain has had its own laws regarding race discrimination and your rights towards protection under the law. (page 2)

⇨ Just under half (48%) of UK adults think that the United Kingdom has become a less racist country in [the last 20 years], with a similar proportion of ethnic minorities (46%) agreeing. (page 3)

⇨ Seven in ten (71%) ethnic minorities think that racist beliefs are still widely held in the UK but are not openly talked about, and 60% believe that racial discrimination is common in the UK. (page 3)

⇨ More than half (58%) of ethnic minorities say that they have been a victim of racial discrimination, while 47% say they have received racially motivated abuse. (page 4)

⇨ Although most of us claim multiple elements to our identity, ranging from our religion to even the local community in which we live, for almost three quarters (72%) of White Britons the country in which they live in is the single most important part of their identity. (page 5)

⇨ Gypsy, Roma and Traveller children were less likely to achieve "a good level of development" in their early years (EYFS) in 2013/14 (19.1% for Gypsy and Roma children, and 30.9% for Traveller children, compared with 61.8% other White children). (page 5)

⇨ A lower percentage of Gypsy and Roma children (13.8%) and Traveller children (17.5%) achieved the GCSE threshold in 2012/13 compared with other White children (60.3%) and the attainment gap widened between 2008/09 and 2012/13. (page 5)

⇨ Gypsies, Roma and Travellers were more likely to report feeling unsafe in prison (46%) compared with other prisoners (33%), and more likely to say they had been victimised by other prisoners (36% compared with 23%) and by staff (40% compared with 27%). (page 7)

⇨ Long-term unemployment among young BAME people has increased by 49 per cent since 2010, while for white people it has fallen slightly. (page 12)

⇨ Although educational attainment is improving among ethnic minorities, those with degrees are two and a half times more likely to be unemployed than their white counterparts, and earn 23.1 per cent less on average. (page 12)

⇨ Research from the thinktank Demos found 61% of ethnic minority children in England, and 90% in London, start year one in schools where the majority of children are from minority groups. (page 13)

⇨ Researchers revealed the most common racial slurs used on [Twitter} included: "p**i", "whitey" and "pikey". However, as many as 70% of tweets using such language were deemed to be using slurs in non-derogatory fashion. (page 14)

⇨ The Anti-Social Media report estimates between 50–70% of tweets were used to express in-group solidarity with "re-claimed" slurs used within ethnic groups. It cites "P**i" as one term becoming appropriated by users identifying themselves of Pakistani descent. (page 14)

⇨ The number of racially and religiously aggravated alleged offences recorded by police in July 2016 was 41% higher than in the same month [in 2015], the Press Association reported. (page 17)

⇨ More than 300 hate crime incidents were reported to a national online portal in the week following the [Brexit] vote – compared to a weekly average of 63, figures from the National Police Chiefs' Council showed. (page 17)

⇨ BAME people are more likely to enjoy their work and have far greater ambition than their white colleagues. 64% of BAME and 41% of white employees in the panel survey said it is important that they progress. (page 27)

⇨ The lack of role models in the workplace is particularly stark for Black Caribbean (11%) and Other Black group (7%) employees, with Chinese and Mixed race employees lacking role models both inside and outside of the workplace. (page 27)

⇨ A report, which analysed research on employment in UK state-funded primary and secondary schools, found that last year just 6% of state primary school teachers and 9.9% of qualified and unqualified teachers in maintained secondary schools were from black, Asian and minority ethnic (BAME) backgrounds. (page 28)

⇨ Just 3% of headteachers in state-funded primary schools and 3.6% in maintained secondary schools are from an ethnic minority groups. (page 28)

⇨ According to a YouGov survey in 2015, 72% of people in Denmark have a negative impression of Roma/Gypsies, compared to 58% of people in Britain and 454% of people in Sweden. (page 33)

BAME

An acronym which stands for Black, Asian and Minority Ethnic backgrounds.

Brexit

A term for the 2016 referendum in which the UK voted to leave the European Union.

Caste

The Indian caste system divides Hindus into different social classes or 'castes'.

Discrimination

Unfair treatment of someone because of the group/class they belong to.

Ethnic minority

A group of people who are different in their ancestry, culture and traditions from the majority of the population.

Gypsies and travellers

Gypsies and travellers have traditionally pursue a nomadic lifestyle which involves moving around from place to place. English gypsies and Irish travellers are protected under the Race Relations Act. This is because they are members of a community with a shared history stretching back over hundreds of years and are recognised by the law as a distinct ethnic minority group.

Harassment

Usually persistent (but not always), a behaviour that is intended to cause distress and offence. It can occur on the school playground, in the workplace and even at home.

Islamophobia

An extreme fear and hatred of Islam and people who follow the Islam faith, otherwise known as Muslims. Since the 11 September 2001 terrorist attacks in New York and Washington and the 7/7 London bombings (7 July 2005), there have been a lot of strong, controversial debates surrounding Muslims and Islam. This has provoked unfair stereotyping of Muslims as people associate their faith with extreme terrorist actions.

Multiculturalism

A number of different cultures coexisting side-by-side, for example within a school or a country.

Racial discrimination

Racial discrimination occurs when a person is treated less favourably because of their colour, race, nationality or ethnic or national origins.

Racial prejudice

The belief and prejudgment that one race is inferior to another. Feeling hatred towards another race just because they are different.

Racism

The belief that one race is superior to another / behaving in a negative or harmful way to someone because of their race.

Racist bullying

Targeting a person because of their race, colour or beliefs. There is a difference between racism and racial harassment: racial harassment refers to words and actions that are intentionally said/done to make the target feel small and degraded due to their race or ethnicity.

Reverse discrimination

When trying to address social inequalities, sometimes reverse discrimination occurs. This occurs when discrimination is directed towards the dominant group in society, in order to favour the usually disadvantaged minority group. People sometimes refer to this as

The Race Relations Act 1976

The Race Relations Act 1976 is concerned with people's actions and the effects of their actions, not their opinions or beliefs. The Act makes it unlawful to racially discriminate against anyone. Racial discrimination is when someone treats a person less favourably because of their colour, race, nationality or ethnic or national origins. Racial discrimination is not the same as racial prejudice. It is not necessary to prove that the other person intended to discriminate against you: you only have to show that you received less favourable treatment as a result of what they did. The Race Relations Act 1976 also aims to promote race equality and good race relations.

Assignments

Brainstorming

⇨ In small groups, discuss what you know about racism?

⇨ What is the difference between racism and ethnic discrimination?

⇨ What is the Race Relations Act 1976?

Research

⇨ The 2017 film *Hidden Figures* is based on the true story of a group of African-American women who worked for NASA to help with the launch of astronaut John Glenn into orbit. Do some research and find out about other inspirational black or African-American figures, choose someone you think your class won't know much about and create a presentation that explores what this person did and how it was influential/important.

⇨ Conduct an anonymous questionnaire amongst your friends, family and peers to find out whether they think racism and religious hatred have increased since the Brexit vote. Ask at least five different questions (remember you're not asking whether people themselves have been racist, but whether they have witnessed it or noticed an increase in the news/media). When you have gathered your results, create some graphs and tables to demonstrate your findings and share with your class as a presentation. Work in pairs if you would like to.

⇨ Who is Malala Yousafzai? Do some research about her and create a presentation that could be used as a school assembly. Perform this for your class.

Design

⇨ Choose one of the articles from this book and create an illustration that highlights the key themes of the piece.

⇨ Imagine that you work for a charity that is campaigning against post-Brexit racism. Create a poster that could be displayed in public places such as bus-stops and tube stations that will highlight your cause.

⇨ Design a poster that summarises UK racism & ethnic discrimination issues.

⇨ Design a storyboard for a Youtube video which highlights the issue of indirect racism. You could choose a setting such as work or school in order to demonstrate your message. If you'd like to take this further and have access to video recording devices, work in small groups and with your teacher to create your video.

⇨ The article on page 37 says that "apps and other online tools are challenging racist attacks". In pairs, design an app or website that will, somehow, help to tackle racism in your community.

Oral

⇨ Create a PowerPoint presentation that explores different types of racism. Use the article on page one for help and try to include some case studies or examples to illustrate your explanations.

⇨ Look at the graph *Proportion of ethnic minorities who have been victims of racial discrimination...* on page three. Which religious group has experienced racial discrimination most frequently? In small groups, discuss why you think this might be.

⇨ Read the article *Muslim women and discrimination in Britain* on page eight. Then, in small groups, write a list of possible Tweets that you could have sent in response to Matthew P Doyle's tweet: "I confronted a Muslim woman in Croydon yesterday. I asked her to explain Brussels. She said 'Nothing to do with me'. A mealy mouthed reply." Your tweets should be polite, reasoned, and aimed at highlighting Doyle's anti-Muslim behaviour.

⇨ As a class, debate the following motion: "Social media should be banned because it encourages racism".

Reading/writing

⇨ Write a one-paragraph definition of the word 'racism' and then compare it with a classmate's.

⇨ Imagine you are an Agony Aunt/Uncle and have received a letter from a young boy asking you 'Why are some people racist?'. Write a letter/email in response.

⇨ Research (see graph on page four) suggests that people view 'politics' as a career that is 'closed off' to ethnic minorities. Write a blog post explaining why you think it is important that ethnic minorities are encouraged to enter this field in particular.

⇨ Write a summary of the article *England's most disadvantaged groups: Gypsies, Travellers and Roma* on page five. Your summary should be no more than three paragraphs.

⇨ Read the Jodi Picoult novel *Small Great Things* and write a book review exploring how the author (a white American woman) has tackled the sensitive subject of racism in America. Consider how the author portrayed the white supremacists as well as the victims, and think about how you felt towards the characters. Finally, consider whether the novel highlighted anything in particular about your own behaviour/attitude to racism.

Acknowledgements

The publisher is grateful for permission to reproduce the material in this book. While every care has been taken to trace and acknowledge copyright, the publisher tenders its apology for any accidental infringement or where copyright has proved untraceable. The publisher would be pleased to come to a suitable arrangement in any such case with the rightful owner.

Images

All images courtesy of iStock except page 6 © Jordan Whitt and page 24 © Simon Davis/DFID.

Illustrations

Don Hatcher: pages 1 & 19. Simon Kneebone: pages 25 & 27. Angelo Madrid: pages 11 & 22.

Additional acknowledgements

Editorial on behalf of Independence Educational Publishers by Cara Acred.

With thanks to the Independence team: Mary Chapman, Sandra Dennis, Jackie Staines and Jan Sunderland.

Cara Acred

Cambridge, January 2017